ALIEN NATION

ALIEN NATION

[THE UNOFFICIAL COMPANION]

EDWARD GROSS

RENAISSANCE BOOKS
Los Angeles

ACKNOWLEDGMENTS
Grateful acknowledgment is made for permission to use the following: Appendix A, "Tenctonese Encyclopedia," by Pete Chambers. Chapter 2, "Creating Feature Film Makeup Effects," was adapted from an article which originally appeared in *Cinefex* magazine, #36, entitled "A Planetful of Aliens," © 1988 by Don Shay.

Library of Congress Cataloging-in-Publication Data

Gross, Edward (Edward A.)
Alien nation : the unofficial companion / Edward Gross.
p. cm.
Includes bibliographical references and Index.
ISBN 1-58063-002-2 (pbk. : alk. paper)
1. Alien nation (Motion picture) 2. Alien nation (Television program) I. Title.
PN1997.A32255G76 1998
791.43'72—dc21 97-51751
CIP

10 9 8 7 6 5 4 3 2 1

Design by Susan Shankin
Distributed by St. Martin's Press, New York
Manufactured in the United States of America
First Edition

CONTENTS

This book is dedicated to
Kenneth Johnson, Gary Graham, and Eric Pierpoint,
the Three Musketeers of *Alien Nation*.

FOREWORD
BY KENNETH JOHNSON

When Fox Television first approached me about creating a series based on their 1988 movie *Alien Nation,* my first response was disinterest. Having created *The Incredible Hulk* for television and then doing the mini-series *"V,"* I felt myself very burned-out on larger-than-life in general, and aliens in particular.

My friend Harris Katleman at Fox really leaned on me to at least look at the *Alien Nation* movie and, out of friendship, I agreed. I was very disappointed with it. I felt that it created a wonderful premise—the world's newest minority—and then very quickly degenerated into *Miami Vice with Coneheads.* I just couldn't get interested in doing *Lethal Weapon* with aliens.

Then I saw one particular scene that turned me around: the Sikes character, played by Jimmy Caan, picked up his alien partner, George Francisco, played by Mandy Patinkin, at George's house. George waved goodbye to his wife and two young children who stood on their front porch. This was his family's only appearance in the picture. It wasn't even a walk-on—it was a wave-on. But I found my curiosity instantly aroused: Who were *they*?

I became intrigued with the notion of what it was like to be them—people from a whole different "world" who suddenly found themselves living in a new society, in a new town, on a new planet, with no choice but to adapt.

The culture clashes and societal impact upon them would be tremendous—and ripe for dramatic exploration. In that instant I saw the myriad directions which *Alien Nation* could take in exploring their lives in this strange new world. The humor, conflict, poignancy, and drama all opened up to me in that moment.

So I went back to Fox and said, "Here's what I'd like to do: a show that explores the cultural impact that our two species have on each other." Fox was apparently so pleased to have me agree to do anything on it, that they immediately acquiesced. Over the next year, however, we continued to have meeting after meeting, in which they wanted to "just make sure that we all understood what the show was about." I finally told them it was about an hour and to leave us alone.

The series became a labor of love for all concerned. My first call was to Eric Pierpoint, who had done a pilot and short-lived series for me a few years earlier, and whom I knew to be a tremendous actor with the necessary measure of Zen to allow him not to go crazy getting in and out of that head every day. I met Gary Graham for the first time in a casting session and immediately knew he was the exact Matt Sikes I was looking for. Gary never let me down. Nor did any of the other cast members, who have become part of my extensive family since we first met in 1989. (Jeff Marcus, who plays Albert the Janitor, and Ron Fassler, who plays Captain Grazer, I had also known from a TV movie the three of us did together in 1981.)

All of the actors were captivated by what we were endeavoring to do on the show, and brought their enormous talents to bear in each episode—contributing, arguing, and always working to make each character in each scene the best it could possibly be.

In addition, of course, the contributions of the writers and producers were paramount to the quality of what we were striving for on *Alien Nation*. My dear friend Diane Frolov got the first call from me and, to my delight, her husband, Andy Schneider, was also available. I had not met Tom Chehak, but had been a big fan of his work. Then Steve Mitchell and Craig Van Sickle became the freshman members of the team. All of them brought great energy and clever creativity to the *Alien Nation* experience. Finally, our pals Harry and Renee Longstreet contributed greatly, in particular on the subsequent TV movies.

The show was not filmed on the ritzy Twentieth Century-Fox lot in Century City, but rather in East L.A., where you had to have a visa to get into the neighborhood. We shot at the Lacy Street Studios, a very funky mom-and-pop operation. The whole thing was like an Andy Hardy movie, "Hey, I've got a barn, let's put on a show!" And we all loved it.

We were crushed when the series was not picked up after the first season (1989–90), because we could all see how much more life it had left in it.

It was a tremendous surprise and delight, three years later, to make the first of the two-hour *Alien Nation* sequel movies. I had been pounding on Fox's door for years, trying to make them realize there was still life in the show, and finally they decided to give it a try—ending up with the highest rated Tuesday night movie they'd had in two and a half years. This of course gave them the inspiration to ultimately buy four more, the most recent of which, *The Udara Legacy*, aired in July of 1997.

Will there be more *Alien Nation* made-for-TV movies after *The Udara Legacy*? Hopefully, yes. However, if this ends up being the last one, we will all have gone out with our heads held high, feeling very proud of the work that we have done and whatever small contribution we may have made to breaking down the walls of intolerance and prejudice in the world. Above all, if the audience is still there and ready for more, so are we.

All of us involved with *Alien Nation* love the program and the opportunity we've had to work together and bring our work before the world's television audience. We're most appreciative of the critics' unanimously positive response and, most importantly, of the fans who kept the show alive for such a long and wonderful time!

INTRODUCTION

My wife, Eileen, loves *Alien Nation*.

You're probably wondering why I'm sharing that little tidbit with you. Well, if you knew how much she dislikes science fiction in general, you'd recognize the significance of that statement.

Alien Nation, one of the most innovative science fiction television series since the original *Star Trek* (1966–69), successfully managed to balance its science-fiction backdrop with the stubborn streak of humanity that makes up the body of producer Kenneth Johnson's work. Based on the moderately successful 1988 feature film of the same name, this television series went far beyond the confines of its cinematic predecessor. It delivered to audiences a weekly examination of the human condition through the eyes of police officer Matthew Sikes (Gary Graham) and his alien Tenctonese partner, George Francisco (Eric Pierpoint).

Alien Nation was a TV cop show with a difference. Like *Cagney and Lacey* (1982–88), it chose to deal with the people element of its stories rather than the crime aspects. No matter how outlandish the situations may have seemed—right down to George Francisco giving birth—the unique cast of characters helped to root them in reality, making it all completely believable. Thus, the series was made completely believable to its viewers, regardless of whether the story line dealt with an investigation of an alien prostitution ring, or a Newcomer's reaction to the deadly game of Russian roulette. Each episode served to further develop the Newcomer race via George Francisco and his family, and took just as much time delving into the background of the Earthling Matt Sikes, evolving him from a bigot to a more complex human involved in an interspecies relationship with a Tenctonese woman. It is probably safe to say that the Sikes-Francisco combination was television science fiction's most potent relationship since *Star Trek*'s Captain James T. Kirk and Mr. Spock.

While critically lauded, *Alien Nation* was canceled by Fox Broadcasting after a single season, 1989–90. For fans of the show the situation seemed hopeless, until four years later when *Alien Nation* lived again in the made-for-TV movie *Dark Horizon*, which has, thus far, spun off four additional two-hour films.

This book is the *only* guide to the entire *Alien Nation* saga, from its initial conception through the latest (1997) TV movie. For making this book possible, and for spending innumerable hours discussing the subject with me, I'd like to thank the following people: Kenneth Johnson, who has continually made himself available to me over the last ten years, and whose creative vision is always an inspiring one; Gary Graham, for the compassion and enthusiasm he has shown for this project, and whose spirituality is also inspiring; Eric Pierpoint, who has somehow gone from interview subject to friend, and with whom conversations have ranged all over the map and far beyond the confines of *Alien Nation*; Brenda Griffin, Ken Johnson's assistant, who has always been there to lend a helping hand, even in the midst of a never-ending series of crises; Rockne O'Bannon, who created *Alien Nation* in the first place and who, I hope, gets the recognition he deserves; and the show's writing staff, consisting of Andrew Schneider, Diane Frolov, Tom Chehak, Steven Long Mitchell, and Craig Van Sickle, who all had the patience to go over every episode with me.

On a personal level, I'd like to thank my editor at Renaissance, James Robert Parish, for his support and belief in this project; Ron Magid and Don Shay for making the chapter on the feature film's makeup effects possible; and Tim Gathercole.

Special thanks go to Pete Chambers of "The Tencton Planet," who provided the encyclopedia presented in this book and who has done more to keep the show alive than any other human or Newcomer on the planet.

I'd also like to thank my sons Teddy, Dennis, and Kevin, who have had to sacrifice *Rugrats* while Daddy watched an episode of *Alien Nation* for the umpteenth time; and my wife, who's always there for me even when I drive her crazy.

And she loves *Alien Nation.*

I still can't get over it.

Edward Gross

1 THE MOVIE

A TWENTIETH CENTURY-FOX Release, 1988.
Color, 96 Minutes. R-Rated.

PRODUCTION CREW

Executive Producer: Bill Borden
Producers: Gale Anne Hurd and Richard Kobritz
Screenplay: Rockne S. O'Bannon
Unit Production Manager: Joan Bradshaw
Director: Graham Baker
Assistant Directors: Herb Adelman, Newton D. Arnold, and Harvey Waldman
2nd Unit Director: Conrad E. Palmisano
2nd Unit Assistant Directors: James Benke and Barbara Ravis
Director of Photography: Adam Greenberg
2nd Unit Director of Photography: Frank Holgate
Camera: Michael A. Benson and Phil Caplan
Production Designer: Jack T. Collis
Editor: Ken Beyda
Assistant Editor: Don Brocha

Associate Editors:	Tracy Granger and Lorraine Salk
Costume Designer:	Erica Phillips
Costume Supervisors:	Linda Serijan Fasmer and Michael Long
Costumer:	Don Bronson
Music:	Curt Sobel
Music Supervisor:	Budd Carr
Music Editor:	Carl Keller
Choreographer:	Sarah Elgart
Casting:	Karen Rea and Frank Warren
Set Design:	John Warnke
Set Decorator:	Jim Duffy
Art Director:	Joseph Nemec III
Makeup:	Zoltan Elek, John Elliott, Michael Mills, and Monty Westmore
Special Effects Coordinator:	Joseph Unsinn
Special Effects:	Jeffrey Machit, John Robles, Michael Stipe, Alan Rifkin, and Richard Lopez
Alien Creators:	Alec Gillis, Shane Mahan, John Rosengrant, Tom Woodruff Jr., and Shannon Shea
Stunt Coordinator:	Conrad E. Palmisano
Production Coordinator:	Janis Benjamin Collister
Location Managers:	Cass Martin, Bruce Rush, and Richard Powell
Linguistics Consultant:	Van Ling
Production Assistant:	Darren Frankel
Sound Recorders:	David MacMillan and Charles Wilborn

ADR Recorder:	Charleen Richards
Sound Effects:	Mark Mangini and Ken Johnson
Sound Re-Recorders:	Don Bassman, Kevin F. Cleary, Richard Overton, and Kevin Carpenter
Sound Mixer:	Bob Schaper
Sound Editors:	Michael J. Benavente, Warren Hamilton Jr., Wayne Allwine, Solange Schwalbe Boisseau, Colin Mouat, Dave Spencer, Lucy Coldsnow, and DonLee Jorgenson
ADR Editor:	Nick Korda
Foley Editors:	Christopher Flick and Peter Tomaszewicz

MAIN CAST

James Caan	(Matt Sykes)
Mandy Patinkin	(Sam Francisco)
Terence Stamp	(William Harcourt)
Kevyn Major Howard	(Rudyard Kipling)
Leslie Bevis	(Cassandra)
Roger Aaron Brown	(Bill "Tuggs" Tuggle)
Peter Jason	(Fedorchuk)
George Jenesky	(Quint)
Jeff Kober	(Josh Struder)
Tony Simotes	(Wiltey)

ADDITIONAL CAST

Michael David Simms	(Human Dealer)
Ed Krieger	(Alien Dealer)

Tony Perez	(Alterez)
Brian Thompson	(Trent Porter)
Frank McCarthy	(Captain Warner)
Keene Young	(Winter)
Don Hood	(Maffet)
Earl Boen	(Duncan Crais)
Edgar Small	(Minkler)
Thomas Wagner	(O'Neal)
Abraham Alvarez	(Mayor)
Diana James	(Ortiz)
Frank Collison	(Bentnor)
Tom DeFranco	(Detective)
Angela O'Neill	(Kristin Sykes)
Kendall Conrad	(Mrs. Francisco)
Brian Lando	(George Jr.)
Tom Morga	(Raincoat)
Reggie Parton	(Mr. Porter)
Jessica James	(Mrs. Porter)
Tom Finnegan	(Natuzzi)
Doug MacHugh	(Victor Goldrup)
Lawrence Kopp	(First Human Cop)
Alec Gillis	(Newcomer in Bar)
Shuko Akune	(Police Secretary)
Stephanie Shroyer	(Female Cop)
Frank Wagner	(Derelict)
Clarence Landry	(Old Man Driver)
Van Ling	(First Newcomer on TV)
Mark Murphey	(Second Newcomer on TV)
Kirsten Graham	(Kid at Burger Stand)
George Robotham	(Boat Captain)
Debra Seitz	(Harcourt's Girlfriend)
James De Closs	(Detective)
Douglas Cameron	(SID Photographer)

Flush with his creative success as story editor of *The New Twilight Zone* in the mid-1980s, writer Rockne O'Bannon was ready for the next challenge. He had come up with a concept initially titled *Outer Heat*, but later changed to *Alien Nation*, which he saw as a hybrid of two distinct movie formats.

"They were the two genres that were of great interest to me at the time," he explains. "First was *Lethal Weapon*, police procedural—a Warner Bros. type of thing, like *Dirty Harry* or *Bullitt*—with a science-fiction scent. What's interesting is that I originally pitched it to two or three places as a television series, not a feature film, and got turned down. Having been story editor on *Twilight Zone* for that year and a half, there was interest in me writing pilots."

His feeling was that *Alien Nation* was a natural for a series, but nobody seemed to see its potential. Perhaps, he muses in retrospect, the idea wasn't developed enough to capture anybody's interest. "I pitched it as a piece about an alien race that gets integrated into regular, modern America," says O'Bannon, who later created the series *seaQuest DSV* which premiered in the fall of 1993. "One of them becomes the first cop detective and he partners with a human. It seems to me that you should be able to get it from that, but people didn't get it at the time.

"This was December/January 1986. I just figured, based on the heat that I had coming off *Twilight Zone*, I would bide my time during hiatus of spring of '87 and get on staff on some other show. So I sat down and wrote it as a spec script, and wrote quickly—like in two months. Then it sold two weeks later and it was filming by October of that same year. It was something like six months from the time I wrote it that it was in production, which happens rarely in Hollywood. I suddenly had a movie career that I aspired to but didn't really expect to happen."

In his script for *Alien Nation*, the background for the story line is that five years earlier a spacecraft containing 250,000 Tenctonese slaves who have been genetically engineered for hard labor had crashed in California's Mojave Desert. As fans of the film and subsequent television series are aware, the Tenctonese, or Newcomers as they're commonly called, are stronger and smarter than the humans on Earth, and generally appear humanoid with the exception of slightly larger skulls that are adorned with a variety of spots. We also learn that they eat raw meat in the form of a variety of animals, their bodies react to salt water as ours would to acid, and the most sensitive areas on their bodies are the armpits. But in O'Bannon's first-draft script their physical appearance is described somewhat differently:

"The aliens are humanoid," he writes, "two arms, two legs, two eyes, a nose, a mouth. None is under six feet tall and their torsos (both male and female) are big and muscular—perfectly suited to heavy labor. Their facial bone structure is quite different than a human's. Most prominent is a heavy eyebrow ridge, giving them a somewhat brutish look. Their skin is a leathery, golden-orange color, and their hair is very coarse and usually black or dark brown, and it seems to encroach on the face more than a human's, making their faces appear smaller than they actually are. This basic description fits all aliens...although, like humans, each has distinctive facial characteristics, heights and shapes, hair styles, etc."

After a brief quarantine on Earth, these beings are given human names (such as Jim Nasium) and integrated into human society. At first humanity is fearful, but ultimately accepts them as Earth's newest minority.

"Many science fiction films have touched on different aspects of alien landings," says O'Bannon. "I thought it would be interesting, instead of building up to the first meeting with an alien race, as in *Close Encounters* [*of the Third Kind*] [1977], if you showed what might happen three years after that. When I sat down to write, and I was thinking budgetarily, I didn't want to write a huge science-fiction piece. I wanted something that was extremely accessible, that made it far more real—the idea that if in fact an 'out there' set of circumstances about a single ship, without any connection to where it came from, were to come into our solar system, all of the initial awe and amazement and fear would eventually subside.

"We tend to be able to adapt to just about anything. Eventually we'd be faced with the conflict of 'What do we do?' The idea is that the ACLU would come to the fore and say, 'We can't just leave them up there in the ship forever. They've been proven not to be dangerous to us, can we put them in a period of quarantine? We need to allow them to integrate with us.' To me that was kind of an interesting jumping-off point."

Alien Nation caught the attention of producer Richard Kobritz, who in turn got Gale Anne Hurd involved for her first producing stint without writer-director James Cameron. Despite the fact that Hurd's company at the time, Pacific West Productions, was receiving upwards of fifty script submissions a week, O'Bannon's premise just leaped out at her.

"It was a story that made sense," says Hurd, "that had all the dramatic beats that are essential to dramatic storytelling. It made me laugh and it touched me. After I read it, I said, 'I want to make this movie.' I was also intrigued by the idea of doing a story about prejudice, like *In the Heat of the Night* [1967], by dramatizing the growing friendship between a tough L.A. street cop and someone—in this case—of a very different race. The Newcomers in this story are the newest boat people. Instead of getting off a boat from El Salvador or Vietnam, they got off a spaceship, but they are still an oppressed race seeking asylum. So we're using the aliens as a parallel to a situation that we confront every day in America."

As the story unfolds, police officer Bill "Tuggs" Tuggle is killed by a Newcomer during a botched robbery. His partner, Matthew Sykes, wants vengeance and to get it he teams up with Newcomer detective George Jetson (ultimately changed to Francisco for legal reasons) to crack the case. En route they become involved in a drug operation involving an alien substance and a Tenctonese named William Harcourt, who plans on cornering the market for himself. Despite their reservations to the contrary, Sykes and Francisco begin gaining a respect for each other which, ultimately, leads to friendship.

Chosen to direct the film by Hurd and Kobritz was British director Graham Baker. "We needed someone who could take a scene and render the visuals intriguing and different," says Kobritz. Hurd adds, "The film needed someone with a vision, and it needed a director who could maximize the performance of the actors. Having known Graham for a couple of years and having seen his work, I thought he was the perfect choice."

Baker for his part was quite intrigued with the basic premise of the aliens, particularly a sequence in which George describes our world as a "green and wonderful land."

"George speaks of our beautiful world and the opportunities it presents," says Baker. "He has come from a place where his people were repressed and used as slaves, and he has been given freedom for the first time. Ironically, of course, that freedom is restricted in the same way many immigrant people's is restricted by lack of education or job opportunities. But it's still better than the situation they came from."

"So George is like a piece of cultural blotting paper. He's soaking up all this information, this new life that's offered to him, and he's like a kid in a candy store," adds Baker, "whereas Sykes is the archetypal hard-bitten and cynical cop. His marriage has ended and he's disillusioned. Probably all he has in life is his friendship with his partner, who's killed at the beginning of the film. But gradually, as a result of being forced to work with George, he begins to see the world a little bit through this alien's eyes, and he becomes more human in the process. Sykes is humanized by someone who's not human."

Cast in the respective roles of Sykes and George were James Caan and Mandy Patinkin, which pleased O'Bannon greatly. "Jimmy Caan has this caged energy," he offers, "and, to me, that played off Mandy very well. Mandy is a very intellectual actor. Just his acting style versus that of Jimmy Caan, whose style is very kinetic, worked really well."

Enthuses Hurd, "Jimmy's wonderful at comedy and he's wonderful at action, and he just seems lived-in and real. He has all the emotional touchstones that the part requires."

"James Caan is truly a fine film actor," says Kobritz. "More important, he's a movie star and his screen energy provides the main thrust for this movie."

Caan describes his character as a basic "Archie Bunker" bigot, for whom Slags—as the Tenctonese are referred to by racists—are one more race he must tolerate. "The only reason I take George on as a partner is that I'm desperately looking for the Slag that killed my partner," he explains. "So George becomes of value to me. But what happens is that I get caught up in a much larger thing, and at the end I'm willing to risk my life for this guy who's beyond the black or Mexican.... I mean, he's a guy from a different world."

Caan ultimately felt frustrated with the role, as his partner, Sergeant Tuggle, was portrayed by a black actor. "The character wavered a little bit from rehearsals," he says. "I wanted him to make Archie Bunker look like Cinderella. Be a real bigot. I mean everybody, every nationality, everything.

You can imagine where the aliens fell on that list. And we talked about it. It was good, because I believe that audiences deserve an emotional reward—and whatever else, whatever the story point is—for the character. At the end, when he's willing to risk his life for these people, and he's gone from A to Z, it's good for the audience, it's good for the actor.

"Of course, I came to work the first day and they'd hired a black guy as my partner. What the hell is that? How could you do that? What does that make me now? What kind of bigot am I? Then my character became an actor who was trying to get through a movie.... Now I'm just a guy who doesn't like this asshole and I'm very narrow-minded about this thing I want to do, and then I get involved in the plot. What really happens is that it makes you believe that the story changes the character instead of the character changing through the story."

O'Bannon agrees with him in principle. "To be honest," he says, "I tend to give the audience credit for being able to pick up subtlety more. In the first draft of the script, Sykes obviously has a disinterest in the Newcomers. It isn't really a hatred born from an Archie Bunker prejudice, it's really just because they're usurping things in his life and encroaching on his comfort zone that he tends to dislike them. I can personally identify with [that] more than an outright Archie Bunker kind of guy. The problem there is you've got an actor who's taking a particular tack, which is fine. He needs to fill the shoes in the way he feels most comfortable, but it was obviously a failure of the production, and the director in particular, in going against what your lead actor is thinking by casting a black in the role. It kind of undercuts Jimmy Caan's take on the character."

According to Mandy Patinkin, he was drawn to the project the minute he read the script, although he was initially concerned about the challenge of playing the role while wearing the Tenctonese makeup designed by Stan Winston's team.

"I talked to the makeup people and to Graham and Gale Hurd about it," he says. "I said I wanted him to be like a baby—I wanted his face to be like a baby's face and I wanted them to express his innocence as much as possible in this massive thing they were going to build. I thought they came up with a very good design, but I was concerned during the initial tests whether I'd be able to express what I was thinking and feeling at all. Then I thought of my children, and especially of my baby, and I realized that what George does, more than most of us, is that he *looks*. The way he gets through this new world is by just trying to be quiet and patient, not saying very much—just watching."

"Mandy's just brilliant," says Hurd. "He brings such warmth and such genuine innocence to the part. He gives a fresh perspective to the portrayal of an alien, which is not quirky—it's very believable."

Makeup was the film's most difficult aspect, with both the producers and Baker realizing that *Alien Nation* would rise or fall based on it. "We weren't doing a picture based on science-fiction hardware," says Kobritz. "The audience should get over the special-effects makeup within the first five minutes of seeing the characters relate to each other. It's a very human picture."

Stan Winston agreed to be a consultant for the early concept stage and brought together a team of designers, sculptors, and makeup artists. The intention was to come close to humanity, but veer off just a little to the left.

"Stan is great at creating characters rather than just creating makeup, and I think that was actually essential in this film," says Hurd. "You couldn't have a mask that spoke. You had to have characters that imparted emotion. Winston's group ultimately came up with a combination utilizing appliances and applied-makeup which allowed the characters absolute freedom in moving their facial muscles."

In contemplating the look he wanted to achieve for the film, Graham Baker decided that it should, essentially, be a night movie, and to capture the contrasts between very dark and very black, he turned to cinematographer Adam Greenberg, who had collaborated with Hurd on the original *Terminator*. Greenberg was well-known for his ability to create dramatic lighting effects in films taking place at night.

Photography on *Alien Nation* began October 12, 1987, on the streets of Los Angeles, and involved shootouts and car chases. The production received special permission to close several blocks of Western Avenue in order to film sequences in the Tenctonese ghetto, nicknamed Slagtown. One of very few remaining historical Los Angeles streetcar "Red Car" tunnels was utilized for a sequence in which Sykes and George meet for the first time. Production designer Jack Collis and his team "modernized" the locale by combining the tunnel's existing graffiti-covered walls with new Tenctonese slogans. More than any other, this tunnel epitomized Slagtown.

Other locales included the San Fernando Valley's Van Nuys Anheuser-Busch plant, which was transformed into the alien refinery where the Tenctonese drug was being manufactured; the Los Angeles Police firing range was filmed at the Police Academy; Club Hollywood doubled as a human bar, Encounters, while a Newcomer bar was shot at Monty's Bar in downtown L.A.

From there the film company transferred over to Los Angeles's Biltmore Hotel, a banquet room of which was used to hold a political fund-raiser at which Harcourt (Terence Stamp) is honored. Next up was Stage 19 at the Twentieth Century-Fox lot, location for a conference room at the Encounters bar and the dressing room of a Tenctonese stripper named Cassandra. Additionally, the final week of production was spent on Stage 19, where a huge tank was constructed for close-ups of the cast during a climactic battle in which George must rescue Sykes from the ocean while precariously hanging onto the rudders of a helicopter. This tank—measuring forty-four feet by twenty-two feet, with a depth of five and a half feet—was erected in a mere three days.

On January 15, 1988, sixty-five days after it started, principle photography was finished on *Alien Nation*. The resultant finished film was only halfway successful on a creative level. While the Tenctonese themselves, and their society, are extremely intriguing, particularly their integration into our society, the second half of the film degenerated into a standard cops-and-robbers film. What should have been the next step beyond *Close Encounters of the Third Kind* became, instead, a retread of the buddy-cop film, such as 1982's *48 Hrs.* and 1987's *Lethal Weapon*. Instead of a thoughtful allegory, viewers were presented with car chases and shoot-'em-ups. As Ken Johnson, who would eventually turn the film into a television series, notes, "It became *Miami Vice with Coneheads*," and as such was fairly forgettable.

The film-viewing public obviously agreed. With a budget of $16 million, *Alien Nation* needed to gross approximately $32 million to break even, but pulled in a lackluster $25 million. The critics were even less kind than the box office. Said *Variety*, "The way Caan and Patinkin play off each other is not unlike the white cop/black cop, straight cop/rebel cop or other oil-and-water pairings in other cop thriller films, except perhaps that these are nearly the dourest duo imaginable.... Caan's explanation to his anatomically-different partner of what a condom is used for is a bright moment. There should have been more of this irreverence."

The *Los Angeles Times*' Kevin Thomas wrote, "Once

[Sykes] gets to know George, who seems modeled after Sidney Poitier's smart, arrow-straight Virgil Tibbs [of 1967's *In the Heat of the Night,* 1970's *They Call Me MISTER Tibbs!,* and 1971's *The Organization*], you know they'll be pals. There's absolutely nothing subtle about this film...." Added *The Hollywood Reporter,* "...the human element is quickly relegated to secondary importance, turning the film into a high-budget episode of *Starsky and Hutch* [1975–79] with prosthetic appliances."

For his part, screenwriter Rockne O'Bannon has mixed feelings regarding the released feature film. "It's the first film produced of my work, so obviously I'm very pleased and proud on a certain level," he says. "But the television series certainly hews much closer to the tone and aspirations I had for it."

O'Bannon's point is obvious when one looks at the first draft of the screenplay. Whereas the audience never meets George's family on screen, they certainly did in O'Bannon's original take on the material. Sykes is reluctantly pulled in to a Tenctonese block party. As O'Bannon notes in the script, "A block party in progress. Five or six alien families from neighboring homes visit the Jetsons' backyard...including grandparents and small children. They talk, they laugh, they play. The side gates of the house are open, inviting all comers. Sykes stands to one side, a glass of water in hand. Although he is the only human present, the partiers make him feel very welcome. He watches the activity around him with fascination...witnesses the love and *humanity* of these creatures."

This scene is just a wee bit different than the final film, and extremely close in tone to Johnson's take on the material.

"The problem," says O'Bannon, "is that Graham Baker wasn't a strong enough presence at the time to push the film through. On the one hand it's gratifying that the studio really seemed to approach it as though it was bulletproof, where they could save money and assign a less expensive director who would do their bidding. John McTiernan was interested in doing it—having just done *Predator*—and he was shot down. He went on to do *Die Hard* and greater fame. Many a night I lay awake wondering what the film would have been like if McTiernan had done it. A stronger director would have fought for a lot more. Graham was not a fighter. He's a great guy, but he's not a fighter. There were lots of changes in the script, little niggly things in it that a stronger director would have shouldered and said, 'No way, you're not touching it.' Ultimately it's the director who makes the movie. For me, that's the failing of the film. Lesson learned for me. Thank God, the TV series came along."

Admittedly bothered that people in general seem to think that Ken Johnson created the concept rather than him, O'Bannon is nonetheless pleased that Johnson was the talent at the creative wheel of the television series.

"I'm really proud to have started it," he says, "and I think Kenny Johnson's taken it much closer to the direction and aspirations I had for it as well. The original script had a lot more heart to it. It was far more interesting than the movie that resulted from it. What interested Kenny for the series was the stuff that kind of got excised from the movie. Look, obviously there are parallels to race relations in 1980s America which were very much at the core of the story that I wanted to tell. There is some of that, but ultimately the way the movie turned out was played on more of a superficial, jokey level. Obviously I tried to infuse a lot of humor into it, but it wasn't at the expense of the richer things. Ken Johnson is someone I've admired since *'V.'* In fact, I used to keep a copy of the script for *'V'* on my desk as inspiration when I first started out on *Twilight Zone*. It was always kind of a thrill to me that he had taken on the mantle of the series."

2 CREATING FEATURE FILM MAKEUP EFFECTS

Science fiction films rarely deal with entire alien populations, since creating hundreds or thousands of extraterrestrials is expensive, time-consuming, and, even today, extremely difficult to do convincingly. Consequently the genre tends to specialize in token representation, with one or two nonhumans on board the Enterprise standing in as a form of economic shorthand for an entire race of alien beings. For this reason, the standard by which all other epic makeup films are measured remains the first—Twentieth Century-Fox's 1968 excursion to the *Planet of the Apes*.

Twenty years after the release of that film, Fox picked up its own gauntlet by presenting *Alien Nation*, a thinly-veiled allegory about racism in which humankind finds itself playing host to thousands of refugees from another planet who have been forced to immigrate to ours. A peaceful, if uneasy, coexistence prevails, though the alien Newcomers are quickly relegated to second-class status. Like other minorities, the aliens live in their own barrios, frequent their own bars and nightclubs, and develop their own underground. And like other minorities in social environments both new and hostile, some engage willingly in crime while others turn to law enforcement. Triggering the plot of *Alien Nation* is a ghetto murder with far-reaching implications. Investigating are two Los Angeles cops—one a racist human played by James Caan and the other an alien officer portrayed by Mandy Patinkin.

To solve the crime—and uncover the monstrous conspiracy behind it—the two must overcome innate mistrust and prejudice and learn to work together no matter how alien their appearances and behavior may seem to the other. As scripted by Rockne O'Bannon, *Alien Nation*—originally titled *Future Tense*—is a science-fictional retelling of *In the Heat of the Night.* In fact, the working title under which it was shot—*Outer Heat*—was a tongue-in-cheek amalgam of *In the Heat of the Night* and *Outer Limits.* Though predominantly an action picture, it is also a socially-conscious throwback to such landmark genre films as *Silent Running* and *Planet of the Apes.*

Co-producing the film was Gale Anne Hurd, whose previous ventures into science fiction include such hugely successful projects as *The Terminator* and *Aliens.* "The screenplay was originally submitted to me on spec—one of twenty or twenty-five that we receive every week. The agency representing it outlined the general idea and asked me to read it very quickly since it was also being sent to other producers at various studios. Ellen Collett, my director of development, and I read it that evening and both of us had the same response—it was a real page-turner and neither of us was able to put it down. Particularly what piqued my interest was the whole approach to the immigrant experience and the extrapolation of that as an allegory in a science fiction setting." Working with coproducer Richard Kobritz, who was already attached to the project—Hurd secured financing through Twentieth Century-Fox and began casting about for an experienced makeup team that could reasonably be expected to bring an alien nation into being. "We knew from the start that it was going to be an enormous undertaking from a makeup standpoint. The primary problem was how to sell an alien race that was humanoid without making it look like people in rubber suits—and how to make it affordable.

We knew there was going to be a lot of makeup application time and removal time—that was a given. But this *is* an alien picture and it was important for us that we not end up with makeup that was prone to smearing and tearing and degraded so quickly after its application that we would spend more time on the makeup than we would on the shooting."

Although several makeup effects companies were considered, the assignment fell—perhaps inevitably—to the Stan Winston studios, where a solid working relationship had already been forged on both *The Terminator* and *Aliens*. Winston himself, however, would not be directly involved. Instead, the design of the aliens and the logistics of running the show would be left to the care of his four top artists—Alec Gillis, Shane Mahan, John Rosengrant, and Tom Woodruff—an approach Winston had employed with success on *Pumpkinhead*, his debut film as a director. The arrangement constitutes an unusual set of golden handcuffs—affording Winston the opportunity to branch out and diversify his talents, while ensuring his effects team continued employment coupled with greater responsibility and increased recognition for individual effort. Without hesitation, the Winston crew members welcomed *Alien Nation* as an opportunity to tackle a show involving strictly foam latex appliance makeups. After years of dealing with mechanical monsters—from *Invaders from Mars* to the *Predator*—the boys in the lab craved nostalgia. They wanted to make their own *Planet of the Apes*. In the process, they got far more than they bargained for—and far less. *Alien Nation* turned out to be the biggest makeup show in twenty years, and the whole thing had to be designed, sealed, and delivered within six months—roughly half the preproduction time allotted to its simian predecessor.

"The four of us—Tom Woodruff, John Rosengrant, Shane

Mahan, and I—were the alien-effects coordinators," Alec Gillis relates. "We were involved in everything from designing and sculpting the aliens to supervising a crew of about thirty people. We sculpted the main characters, supervised the molding and production of their appliances, and oversaw the sculpting of the secondary and background characters." After several meetings with Gale Anne Hurd, director Graham Baker, and Stan Winston, the alien coordinators began making dozens of preliminary design sketches. "At first we went off and made our own sketches," Tom Woodruff recalls. "Then we got together and compared drawings and did tracings of certain parts in order to put together a composite character. Most of the designing on paper fell to Alec Gillis, John Rosengrant, and me, while Shane Mahan worked out some problems in clay."

"We went through a lot of design phases," Gillis adds. "I think the earlier designs tended to be more outrageous, but it was decided that the look shouldn't be too 'over the top.' The script described the aliens as having leathery skin leaning toward the reptilian—and none of them were under six feet tall, so at first they were all hulking creatures. It's hard to say how many designs we did—maybe six different designs on paper and another five when we started sculpting, narrowing it along the way, taking some of the lumps and bumps off until it was smooth and refined. We always wanted to create something that looked as if it might be another variation on the human species with a bit of extra texture. We wanted to make the features a little cruder, and we tried various things such as moving the nostrils and other features to slightly different places." Resisting attempts to accentuate the alien elements, Baker and his producers held firm in their insistence that the Newcomers be made to look as human as possible. For the makeup crew, artistic interpretation was not the only issue involved. "If for no other reason," John Rosengrant admits, "we felt that the alien approach would be easier because the appliances would be thicker and therefore simpler to make and apply."

More concerned with concept than convenience, the director and producers continued de-emphasizing the alien aspects and insisted upon greater subtlety. "We wanted the aliens to be more like a different ethnic race than like lizard people," Hurd explains. "That was a very conscious decision. We didn't want our audience thinking, 'Gee, look how different these aliens are.' Rather, after about five minutes we wanted the audience to accept them as different from us, but not *so* different that no one is buying the story line. We wanted the aliens to be characters—not creatures."

Based on approved design sketches, Shane Mahan and Shannon Shea commenced sculpting a series of masks—three male and three female—to be worn by background characters in the numerous crowd scenes. Even here there were some differences in interpretation. "Our clay models started out a bit more frightening looking than they ended up," says Mahan, "and they had a lot more texture. But the producers and director thought they were a bit too ugly. We went through a phase where the males were going to have spines on top of their heads—kind of like a rooster's comb—and when they got angry, these spines would raise up. That would've required a mechanical headpiece, and Graham Baker thought it was a little too extreme so we went with smooth heads instead." Even without the rooster combs, the background characters turned out to be more alien than the featured principals. "The background designs look most like our original characters," Woodruff explains. "They have heavier brows and heavier skin texture that looked more leathery, and there were more pronounced lumps on the backs of their heads. After we went into production on these masks, Graham Baker decided that he wanted the aliens to look even more subtle, so we streamlined the design once we started doing the principal characters. At that point we had already made about a hundred background masks, but we decided to go ahead and use them since they were going to be far away in most of the shots and would not cause a problem."

"Ultimately, the aliens had very smooth skin and almost featureless faces," says Mahan. "Their eyebrows were flattened, their noses were broadened, they had no ears and their heads were larger than a human's. The director didn't want them to look menacing since they're basically benevolent creatures. He wanted the makeups to be subdued in order to allow the character of the actor to read through the rubber pieces." Baker's insistence upon greater and greater subtlety was rooted in his fear that audiences would be alienated by the characters instead of identifying with them. "He wanted people to immediately take a liking to the aliens," adds Rosengrant. "Since they're on screen for most of the movie and most of them are sympathetic, I don't know that I completely agree with his desire to make them as human as possible—but I have to admit they worked. When I went out to the set and saw the aliens walking around, I got a really neat feeling because they actually seemed like a real race of people."

As the alien-effects coordinators struggled to finalize concepts and commence full-scale production, attendant efforts were underway to enlist a top-notch makeup artist to supervise the application of the alien prosthetics on set. At the top of Gale Anne Hurd's list was Zoltan Elek—a veteran makeup artist whose work with Michael Westmore on *Mask* had earned an Oscar in 1985. "Obviously the only way a makeup design will work on set is if the person who is applying it every day and touching it up can carry out the intent of what has been planned and developed and tested—perhaps even prior to his or her involvement. Zoltan came recommended by Stan Winston—they had worked together on numerous occasions. In fact, we had tried to get him on *Terminator*, but he was doing *Mask* at the time. When we started this project, Zoltan was working on *Max Headroom*, but he was able to come in and consult with us while we were designing the makeups and discuss with us application problems that we might encounter."

Though he enjoyed a longstanding working relationship with Winston—most recently, at the time, on *Monster Squad*—Elek balked at what he perceived to be another monster movie. At this point in his career, what he wanted to do were character makeups—which Hurd insisted was exactly what she and Graham Baker had in mind for *Alien Nation*. Not easily swayed, Elek had to see for himself. "The first time I went to Stan's lab to look at the alien designs, I was not too hot on them," Elek admits. "*Monster Squad* was fun, but I didn't want to do another film like that right away and this show looked to me like another monster movie. When I went in to see Gale, I told her, 'I really don't know if I want to do this show unless the aliens are made to resemble humans more closely—which means much more delicate work for me than making monsters.' Gale insisted that the designs were being changed and I told her, 'In that case, I'm available.' Ultimately she and the director kept changing things until they almost pushed the aliens too far in the opposite direction—they're almost too human. Their facial structure is completely different, but they still remind us so much of ourselves that we can believe them—which is how I saw them when I first read the script." Ironically, the very changes Elek insisted upon were to cause him considerable aggravation during the shoot, creating one of the most difficult challenges of his career.

Once a generic alien concept was agreed upon and finalized, each of the alien-effects coordinators selected a specific area to supervise from beginning to end. Shane Mahan opted to handle the Sam (eventually George) Francisco makeup for lead actor Mandy Patinkin. John Rosengrant took the supporting character of Cassandra—a female alien and exotic dancer played by Leslie Bevis—and also supervised the small alien son of Francisco. Tom Woodruff selected the character of William Harcourt—an evil alien drug trafficker fronting as a respectable businessman—played by Terence Stamp. Late in the film Harcourt overdoses on the mind- and body-altering drug he is attempting to manufacture and peddle to his own people—necessitating a transformation suit, which became Alec Gillis's primary responsibility. Though certain areas were overlapped and the full assignment extended far beyond the principal characters, the supervisory compartmentalization eased the workload considerably.

Sculpting for the principal makeups was technically straightforward. A full-head lifecast was taken of each actor, over which the alien appliances were fashioned in clay. Virtually all of the makeups were conceived originally in seven pieces—one each for the neck, chin, and forehead, one for each cheek, a combined nose-and-upper-lip piece, and a headpiece encasing the ears and the back of the head. The challenge for the artists was to accurately capture the personality of each actor in his or her own makeup. "That was one of the most important things for us," Mahan insists. "We wanted the audience to be able to recognize the actors immediately. They were all so good, it would have been a shame to cover them up completely." With appliances covering nearly every major facial feature, the task was not as simple as it might seem. "We were very fortunate," remarks Gillis, "in that a lot of the actors had great faces to begin with. The actor who played Trent Porter, for example—Brian Thompson—was a really rugged guy, so he came off looking like a really rough character. On the other hand, Kevyn Major Howard—who played Harcourt's murderous henchman—had very delicate, boyish kind of features, so we used that quality to create a creepy juxtaposition."

Even with the alien physiognomy firmly established, other changes continued to plague the makeup unit. When Zoltan Elek came in to do his first makeup test, he argued insistently that the alien coloration should be much closer to human tones than the yellowish pigment already established. "Stan didn't agree with me fully in the beginning," Elek recalls. "He felt the aliens should be a totally different color than the humans, with a lot of yellows, blues, and grays. To me, that scheme was too monstrous—in fact, we ended up using it on the Harcourt monster at the climax. But when I did the first makeup test—and this is one of the reasons I love Stan—I had a long talk with him and convinced him to give my ideas a chance. He said, 'Okay, you're doing the test, so this whole coloring thing is in your hands.' I did my first makeup test on Brian Thompson, who plays the son of an old alien killed in a liquor store shooting. My first color scheme came out too warm—he ended up looking like a redneck from Texas—but the producer, director, and cameraman liked the general concept, even though they wanted it toned down. Luckily, this meant I was on the right track from the first test. Unfortunately, this blew off Stan who already had some ninety background masks finished and painted. The masks were of a yellowish color, while the tone we went with looked more orange to the naked eye and photographed exactly like human skin."

As any makeup artist will attest, the most difficult prosthetic makeup is one worn by a beautiful woman who must still look beautiful. In the history of special makeup effects, only a handful of these makeups have ever been successfully handled—for example, the fine work by Tom and Bari Burman on Nastassia Kinski in *Cat People* and Anjelica Huston in *Captain Eo*. Now John Rosengrant can add his transformation of actress Leslie Bevis into the alien stripper Cassandra to this select number of well-realized female characters. "It was hard work," Rosengrant affirms. "Going into it, creating the female aliens seemed like it was going to be much easier than it was. To duplicate the softness of a woman's face and skin texture—first in clay and then in foam latex—became a very tough job. You would think just duplicating a female's face would be simple, but it was one of the most demanding sculptures I have ever had to do. Making a beautiful woman beautiful gave me a helluva time."

Rosengrant made his first clay sketch over the most unlikely of lifecasts. "I took an old cast Stan had lying around of Mary Tyler Moore and tried to give her face an alien look without making it ugly. I gave her a different, more pronounced bone structure and also flared and swept back her nostrils. Graham Baker took a look at my clay sketch and felt it was the right direction to go in, so I just happened to fall into doing the female alien." Once Rosengrant was able to sculpt on Leslie Bevis's own lifecast, Baker requested that the female alien be made even more subtle. "I must have resculpted her three times just to get the right smoothness and a nice fleshy look. I kept bringing the pieces closer to a human face, making changes in the nose, the cheekbones, everywhere, to make it very subtle. Once it was cast, we did a makeup test which just was not satisfactory, so I went back and made some more changes. Fortunately, even though we were working on a very tight schedule, I had a few weeks left before my character started working, so I was able to do it the way I like to see things done—I made a prototype, ironed out the problems, and then remade it for real. When we did the second makeup test, everything was fine and dandy."

Another makeup test for a sequence in which the Cassandra character does an exotic striptease did not go so well. "We constructed an entirely new body for her out of appliances," Gillis says. "We made a set of breast pieces to enlarge her bust, a stomach piece with a navel that went down just below her belt line, new shoulder blades, a more protruding spine and a small tail. It was made entirely of foam latex, and the test makeup—applied to an actress other than Leslie Bevis—really looked great. At first Graham was really pleased with it, but after mulling it over he decided the safest thing to do was not to use it. He felt the makeup was becoming too grotesque and would take away from Cassandra's beauty. He was very wary about turning the audience off from these characters, so the suit fell by the wayside. They ended up just putting body makeup on her—and since she has a nice body, it worked fine."

Based on the experience of creating the Cassandra facial makeup, Rosengrant supervised the sculpting—by David Anderson and John Blake—of two other minor female characters. In a similar vein, he oversaw the production of the alien makeup for child actor Brian Lando—playing Francisco's son—another extremely difficult assignment. "Once again we were faced with the problems I had doing the female makeup—children are very soft and smooth and textureless. Fortunately we were able to start with a lifecast of the actor, which gave the proper proportions—the shape of the skull, the small nose, and the puffy little cheeks. It was a matter of taking distinguishing alien features and scaling them down to fit a child's face."

After the principal makeups were sculpted, each had to be molded again and again. Mandy Patinkin, for example, had to have enough prosthetics for three months of shooting—some ninety sets of appliances. "We were fighting a time crunch," Mahan relates. "In order to make all of the pieces required, I had to duplicate every single positive and negative mold part for each appliance many times. There was no way we could have made all the pieces we needed with just one set. I can't even begin to give an accurate count of how many molds there were, but we must have ended up with at least seventy individual molds—just for Mandy. His makeup was the most extreme case—for that one I had to make six or seven molds for each piece—though Terence Stamp's molds also had to be duplicated a few times, as did many of the other characters'." Remaking prosthetic molds is an art in itself, requiring great precision to ensure that the duplicates are as accurate to the sculpture as the originals. In order to ensure against the generational loss of size and detail that would occur if appliances from the original molds were cast, Mahan injected liquid Roma clay into a silicone mold of the original sculpture. He then finessed his clay press, carefully blending it down onto Patinkin's lifecast to ensure that the thickness of the duplicate pieces would match those of the originals. "If the thickness was not exactly the same on the original and the duplicate pieces, Mandy's face might appear to swell and shrink from shot to shot. Once the clay press was touched up, I recapped each of the pieces with a stone mold. Making each piece six times took quite a long while to do."

Heavily taxed to supply even one set of appliances per day for each principal actor, the Winston crew found their workload multiplied as production began and the on-set application crew—headed by Zoltan Elek—began demanding backup copies for each day's shooting. "Because actors need breaks and because of problems with timing," Mahan explains, "the on-set guys requested double makeups—which meant we had to send out two sets at a time instead of one. That was difficult, but we did it somehow. There was no time to do anything extra, however. Whenever there were little glitches in the pieces—like air bubbles, for example, where we would normally not use those pieces—we would have to send them to the set anyway. It was either that or nothing."

"One of the challenges of this job," Gillis adds, "was the limited amount of time for research and development. Under normal conditions any one of these characters would have taken several months to do. On this project, we had to break our schedule down and allow just two-and-a-half weeks to get each character into full production—including duplicating the molds. There was no time to go back and deal with problems. We really had to crank them out. The worst part was that everything we did had to go before the camera as it was. It was really a rough show from that point of view." Hard-pressed as always, it soon became apparent to the effects coordinators that there would not be time to create individual character makeups for day players. Taking their cue from a system Kenny Myers developed for *Return of the Living Dead: Part II*, the alien unit decided to use mix-and-match makeups on bit actors. "We would grab a head from this one and a chin from that one and so on until we'd put something together for each character," Mahan recalls. "The system had its obvious problems, but it worked okay—especially when we had our big street scenes where there were supposed to be hundreds of aliens. We wanted to have a nice gradation between our principal characters and our background characters."

The greatest single technical failing of *Planet of the Apes* is the lack of gradation between the wonderful principal makeups and the mediocre background masks—a problem the *Alien Nation* crew sought to avoid. "We had what we referred to as 'A-B-C-D' makeups," Gillis explains. "The 'A' makeups were those custom designed for the principal actors, while the 'B' makeups were mix-and-match where we would recombine pieces from other actors to create a new character. The 'C' and 'D' makeups were just background masks. Our 'D' masks—the ones furthest from camera—were overhead slip latex masks incapable of changing expression. The 'C' masks, however, were made of foam latex and could be glued down to get some expression from the characters in the middleground."

Soon appliances and masks were being manufactured on a production-line basis to ensure that the vast demand for pieces would be met. "That was the biggest chore," Mahan affirms, "trying to keep up with the demand. We had a mass production system going on where one person would be assigned to do all the heads, for example. We would pull the pieces out of the oven, fix them up, paint them, and have them ready for pickup that afternoon to be taken to the set. The pieces were barely cold when Zoltan and his crew applied them." In this type of high-speed mass production, the headpieces promised to be the Achilles' heel that might bring the whole manufacturing process to a standstill. Making those pieces took about as long as any other, but painting them was another matter. Mike Spatola headed up the painting crew charged with maintaining consistency on the many hundreds of prosthetic pieces churned out for the show. Although the aliens were hairless by design, the coordinators decided that they should have spotted skin where hair would be on a human. Thus each alien headpiece had to have a custom-painted spotting pattern that matched with precision to every other headpiece made for that particular character. The situation looked grim until someone came up with a revolutionary idea. "We made vacuformed shells off a plaster copy of each head appliance," Gillis reveals, "then cut out holes in the plastic pieces where the spots would be. It really saved us a helluva lot of time, especially since we could not reuse the headpieces as we had hoped. There was no way to remove them in one piece, so we had to produce a new headpiece for each day's shooting. These templates really saved the day, and I think there's a lot of potential uses for them in other jobs as well."

During one of his first tests, Elek added another unexpected element. "Even though the aliens were supposed to be bald, with only those patterns on their heads, I felt that if we did not add some other texture they would look too rubbery. Stan was one hundred percent against the idea until I tried using chopped hair, which produced just a very slight stubble. In fact, when the characters were photographed from the front or the side, you could not actually see the hair—you could only sense a kind of texture on their heads. If the aliens were backlit you could see it, but even then all you could detect was a little fuzz."

Sadly, some aspects of the alien makeups had to be discarded because they were too uncomfortable for the actors or too time-consuming for the lab crew to make. Contact lenses for the aliens were immediately ruled out because of the large numbers of actors involved, all of whom would have to be specially fitted. Expense aside, it was concluded that the actors would have enough trouble wearing the elaborate makeups without the added burden of lenses. Also quick to fall by the wayside were special hand appliances designed to be muscular in appearance and cover each actor's hands and forearms. Though a production line was begun to start manufacturing the pieces, ultimately these too were discarded to minimize performer discomfort. Instead of appliances, each actor's hands were covered with makeup and detailed on the backs with a few spots."

As the work progressed, Zoltan Elek began to realize with growing anxiety that in asking for subtler makeups, he had unintentionally created an almost impossible task for himself. "Ninety percent of each makeup was totally free of wrinkles or large features—they were very smooth. With appliance makeups that smooth, it meant that I could not afford to make any mistakes along the blending edge as I applied it because any error would break up the smoothness of the surface and betray the fact that it was a makeup. Also, the way the makeups were broken down was very complex and each piece went on in an unusual way. During the tests we very carefully developed a system of applying each piece. It took a long time and a lot of sweat to figure this system out." Due to the special difficulties the alien appliances presented, each makeup artist Elek hired had to be trained to apply the complex prosthetics. "This was definitely not a regular appliance show. Each time I brought in extra help I had to have them come in a day early to watch how the makeups were done and to explain everything so the next day they would know what to do. Because of the complexity of the makeup, it was impossible for even the best makeup artist in the world to come in cold and do it." At first reading, Elek failed to realize just how many aliens would be called for by the script. "Once the makeups were finalized during the tests, I realized I had no idea how we were going to handle all the people we had to make up—especially since we had to train everyone to do this. When we were shooting both first and second unit, I had to have seventeen makeup artists—including two hairdressers and a body-makeup person—in order to handle the workload."

The intensely demanding nature of the alien makeups created one unforeseen and exciting benefit for the entire production. "Every single makeup artist who came to help us wanted to come back, because where else could they get this much experience? John Elliot, Michael Mills, and Monty Westmore were my principal assistants, but everyone on my crew wanted to have a chance to try making-up each character because they all turned out to have their own unique set of problems. Makeup artists love that. It's the best way to learn—when you have to try different things and use all your skill to figure out how to solve a problem immediately. Many times we did not even have time to test the makeups—we just had to do them—but that was the fun of it."

When the effects coordinators discovered how complicated their makeups were to apply, they tried to find ways to simplify them by condensing the number of pieces. "Since the overlapping pieces did not move as we had hoped," Alec Gillis notes, "we ended up combining several pieces to make one big appliance that would cover half of an actor's face. Thus we were able to condense many of our original seven-piece makeups into four pieces—two large face pieces in conjunction with the headpiece and the neckpiece. Of course, we had to remold the makeups to do it. Just when we realized we could get away with doing the makeups this way, Shane finished his work on Mandy Patinkin's prosthetics. Things got so fast and furious that we never had a chance to redesign that makeup, so Mandy always had to wear the more difficult seven-piece makeup."

As unfortunate as this was for Patinkin, it was many times worse for Elek who had the dubious honor of applying those complex pieces day after day. Three-and-a-half to four-and-a-half hours per application were required to complete the process, which Elek proclaimed to be the toughest make-up job of his career. "I first applied Mandy's baldcap, which covered his hair and provided an anchor to secure the head-piece. Next I applied a full neckpiece which extended from his shoulders up to his chin. Once that was in place, I attached the headpiece which covered the back of his head and ears, ending a little higher than his hairline in front. Since his ears were glued in practically airtight, sometimes I would have him test the makeup by shutting his lips, pinching his nostrils, and blowing air out of his ears. If he felt a leak anywhere, I knew the headpiece was not secure. The chin piece was next. That ended just below his lip line—which is a hard blend to accomplish. The toughest piece I've ever worked with was Mandy's nose piece. It was so thin and the rubber was so soft that if I put the adhesive on and slipped by a hair as I was pressing the piece down, I would push a wrinkle into it that I would never be able to get out—I'd have to throw the whole thing away. It was so tough that even though I applied it more than sixty times, I always said, 'Oh God, please be with me now'—and I really meant it. Finally I applied the forehead piece.

"Blending these seven pieces together seamlessly was the hardest part of the whole job, because the key to these makeups was their smoothness. Once they were blended perfectly, I could not afford a single mistake in the coloring because it would read right away—like a blemish on a clean sheet of paper. The toughest blend of all was between the cheek piece and Mandy's eyes. The skin around his eyes had about three times more texture than the rubber appliances, so it was like trying to blend a sheet of plastic onto a bed of sand. Even after it became routine, it was still difficult to pull off. I solved the problem by using colors to give a texture to the rubber pieces, while around his eyes I used five or six colors to block his texture. The goal was to create a uniform texture all over his face that was not seen, but felt. It was a tough job."

Perhaps the most difficult aspect of the task was the need to subject Mandy Patinkin to this grueling ordeal nearly every day of the sixteen-week shoot. As much as possible, Elek attempted to ease the actor's discomfort—though in at least one instance his efforts backfired. "Early in the show, Mandy's baldcap was so tight that it gave him a headache, so we began stretching the baldcaps so they would slip on easier. But since the whole reason for the baldcap was to provide an anchor for the headpiece, when the baldcap was loose, so was the headpiece. I'll never forget one Friday when we were shooting in a tunnel downtown. Mandy was the only alien actor working and the makeup was unusable, thanks to that loose baldcap. Whenever he looked up, a giant wrinkle ran across his forehead. When the person who helped me apply the makeup saw that, he walked away—but I could not. I had to face the director and the producer and everybody else who asked, 'Why is his face doing that?' I was the one who had to tell them, 'Sorry, guys, I can't do a thing about it because it's all one piece by now.' In order to correct the problem, I would have had to take the whole thing off and start over again. Fortunately, the moment I told them that, it started to rain. I tell you, I must be the best raindancer in the world, because I prayed for it to keep on pouring and it did. They had to call off the whole day because of weather." That night, as much as he hated to, Elek had to lay down the law to Patinkin. "I explained to him that he had to understand it was nothing personal, but I could not afford to do that kind of thing anymore. From then on, you should have seen the baldcap on him—it was like a helmet. We nailed that makeup down so well that no matter what he did to it, it never loosened up."

Although *Alien Nation* turned out to be a much more demanding show for both Elek and Patinkin than either had anticipated, neither of them lost their sense of humor—though there was generally little time to express it. "I was doing

Mandy's makeup for three or four weeks when his two little sons—who were five and three years old—came out to visit the set. One of the kids watched the whole makeup, and at the end he said, 'Daddy, I thought aliens were blue.' We all laughed. When Mandy was done shooting, I painted him blue."

Laughs were few and far between for Elek, especially when he found himself having to deal with some of the less-than-perfect appliances supplied by the overworked lab crew. "They were making headpieces twenty-four hours a day because they were so big and time-consuming to produce and because we needed a new one for each character every day. For that reason, pieces would sometimes come from the lab with bumps and air bubbles here and there. Since the lab was so overloaded, they could not always supply my crew with the best possible pieces. They had no choice—which meant we had no choice. When these defective pieces came in, my first reaction was to run to the phone and say, 'You guys really did a damn good job on me again.' But then they would remind me that they only had twelve hours to make a piece that normally took fourteen hours and it had been the best they could do. I knew they were right, but I would go back to work fuming because *I* was the one who had to look the director in the eye and say, 'That's all we have.'"

It was with no little irony that the day Alec Gillis arrived on set to play a bit part as an alien his appliance pieces did not fit. "We got the pieces from the lab that day," Elek recalls, "and we all sat down and went to work like we normally did. All of a sudden the two people who were doing Alec realized something was wrong—the two cheek pieces were about an inch-and-a-half too small. I was right in the middle of my usual makeup on Mandy, but I looked at the pieces and there was no question—they were unusable and we had no backups. Then I remembered that we were going to have a new character on the next day who was supposed to wear one of the mix-and-match makeups and I had told the lab guys to send out some extra pieces so we could make the best fit. I said, 'Get those pieces and use them on Alec. That will give us twenty-four hours to figure out what we're going to do tomorrow.' So we sorted through the pieces until we found some that worked, and stuck them on." After the fact, it was found that the original pieces had not been defective as presumed—merely mislabeled.

Gillis was not the only effects coordinator to appear in a bit part. "Almost all of us got a chance to do a small part," says Tom Woodruff, "so Alec Gillis appeared in a bar scene while John Rosengrant and Richard Landon were at one of the drug deals. I was supposed to be one of the first aliens you see—a busboy at a bar—but my part was reshot because the executives at Fox thought I looked too much like Mandy Patinkin. Although I was a little disappointed, I really got a kick out of being in makeup again. I had not done that since I was about fourteen, and it was a real treat to have someone else put the pieces on."

Actors rarely enjoy wearing full prosthetic makeups, but nothing prepared Elek and his crew for Terence Stamp's incredibly difficult behavior. "When Terence came in to be made up for the first time," says Elek, "he almost broke his contract because he insisted no one had informed him that his entire head would be covered by that makeup—he said he was claustrophobic." Having expressed his displeasure in unequivocal terms, the actor nonetheless submitted to makeup artist John Elliott, whom Elek had assigned to do his application. "I had to put John on Terence because I was busy doing Mandy every day. Since they had a lot of scenes together, I knew I would never be able to handle them both. At the start I said to John, 'Be careful with Terence. Feel him out each time he comes in. If he's in a good mood, talk to him; if he isn't, don't. Get him out of that chair and to the set as quickly as possible. Then after they shoot, clean him up right away and let him go.' And that's exactly what we did." To accommodate Stamp, his scenes were invariably shot as soon as he arrived on the set in makeup. "The director wanted to shoot Terence as quickly as he could. Unfortunately, that meant that a lot of the other actors—including Mandy—had to wait around, sometimes for hours, before they got in front of the camera. Some of my actors didn't get to work at all."

Despite the concessions, Stamp's cooperation became increasingly more difficult to obtain—much to the chagrin of Alec Gillis and John Rosengrant who were tasked with achieving Harcourt's transformation and ultimate disintegration. "It was really sad," says Gillis. "By the end of the show, Terence was so sick of the makeup that he refused to wear the transformation suit we had made specifically to fit him. As a result, we had to put our transformation appliances on a stuntman who looked nothing at all like Terence—he had a much thinner face. We put the pieces on anyway, but I personally don't think the makeup looks as good as it would have if Terence Stamp had worn it."

The Harcourt transformation occurs during the waterfront climax of *Alien Nation* when the drug kingpin—in a moment of defiance and desperation—swallows an apparently fatal quantity of his own narcotic. Little do the ambulance attendants realize, however—as they carry away the seemingly lifeless body—that aliens who overdose on this particular drug later transform into a faster, more ferocious and dangerous breed. When Francisco and Sykes get an emergency call, they rush out to the docks where they find the ambulance overturned, its doors ripped from their hinges, and the attendants dead. The Harcourt monster is loose.

Surprisingly, the actual transformation is handled entirely off-screen—a welcome respite from the overdone puffing bladders and spastic cabling that have characterized nearly every horror film since *The Howling*. "Harcourt is revealed lurking in the darkness, already transformed," Gillis remarks, "so there is no actual scene where you see his body swelling. I think it's better that this was treated in a dramatic way—personally, I'm tired of transformations. I think there have been some excellent ones in the past, but who needs to see it anymore? We were much more interested in the final result than in watching it happen." Although the shooting script described the transformed Harcourt as a grotesque, oversized version of the alien design, like most of the effects in the film, this too was softened. Consequently, the makeup became about as subtle as a monster makeup can be and still be called a monster makeup. "The way the script was written had us thinking about getting a huge actor like Kevin Peter Hall to play the part, but that was all scaled down by the time we got around to sculpting the transformation suit. We did not go for a giant Lou Ferrigno 'Hulk'—it was more subtle than that. We were somewhat limited by the fact that the transformation had to occur in the period of an hour-and-a-half or so between the time he overdoses and the time he faces Patinkin and Caan by the docks. Basically, I just exaggerated everything that was there in Stamp's normal-phase makeup, only I made it more ferocious and bestial. I gave him a tumorous-looking head, which implied some radical internal change. His skull was lumpier, his facial features exaggerated, and his skin texture was more leathery. In my mind, he's a dead man—it's his last rush. It's as if he's become this psycho junkie whose body has gone though this transformation and all this pain, and who's probably going to die anyway."

Harcourt finally meets a well-deserved end, after a showdown with Sykes results in his total immersion in sea water—which, it has been established, dissolves alien flesh like acid. The disintegration effect was handled in two stages. Stage one involved a dissolving head and body, accentuated with on-stage effects rigged by Zoltan Elek. Stage two featured a nearly fleshless artificial arm which needed to be thrust up out of the water. The disintegration heads and bodysuits were supervised by John Rosengrant and constructed by a crew that included Grant Arndt, Greg Figiel, Mike Trcic, and Andy Schoeneberg. "I ended up blocking out the first stage of the disintegration as he begins to dissolve," Rosengrant recalls. "It was pretty straight-forward stuff—just a question of dissolving his skin to reveal bone and muscle. It was fun because we all got into doing something that was really wild and distorted." While the dissolving makeup had to look extreme, it also had to appear realistic within the limits of the alien anatomy Winston's crew had designed. "We wanted to avoid the amorphous 'blob-of-blood' look you see in so many of these slasher and monster pictures. We wanted to be able to see Harcourt's bone structure rather than just the glob hanging off of it. Of course, we did use methocel slime to make it wet and nasty-looking, but the basic understructure was rooted in anatomy. We had already developed a somewhat alien anatomy for these characters, done mainly with wardrobe, to suggest that they had a different shoulder-bone structure and were barrel-chested. When it came time to do the disintegration, we just used our knowledge of this alien anatomy in order to distort it so that we could make Harcourt appear to dissolve the way he really would. We used forensic medicine books to anchor the makeup in a recognizable reality, even though it is extreme and bizarre."

Making a close-fitting appliance appear to be eaten away

is one of the more difficult makeup illusions. "On Harcourt," Rosengrant continues, "the appliances were built up a lot over his cheekbones, but they became very thin on the hollow of his cheeks in order to give it a more dramatically cut and sunken look. We wanted quite a bit of his skull to be showing through, and we made it intentionally asymmetrical because injuries do not often occur symmetrically in nature. The transformation bodysuit was sculpted by Greg Figiel and Mike Trcic on a cast of Terence Stamp's body—who never even wore it. Once it was molded, a spandex suit was placed over the body form and that was put in the mold while the foam rubber piece was run around it. Once the foam was cured, all the pieces meshed right into the spandex, which gave it strength, prevented it from tearing, and made it very flexible." Because stuntman Terry Jackson—who eventually wore the suit—was working in water, several backups had to be made to allow those already immersed to dry out before they were needed again. "The makeup really survived pretty well in the water," Gillis remarks. "We sprayed it with a urethane coating which acted as a bit of a sealant, but there was really no way to effectively stop the water from leaking into the foam latex. We just had to squeeze the bodysuit out at the end of the day and dry it off. So long as we treated it carefully, we could use it over and over."

For Harcourt's facial disintegration, the alien-effects coordinators came up with a foam-rubber base makeup to provide the essential structure, then superimposed a layer of gelatin appliances that served as the skin which was to dissolve via an ingenious system devised by Zoltan Elek. "We dug out chunks from the foam rubber pieces, filled the holes with Bromo Seltzer, then laid the gelatin appliances over the whole thing and colored them so you could not see the holes below. Once the stuntman, the cameramen, and everyone else was in position, we took a large syringe filled with hot water and injected it into each of the Bromo Seltzer pockets as the cameras started rolling. As the Bromo Seltzer started to fizzle, the hot water began eating its way through the gelatin skin and his face appeared to bubble and melt." The effect took several hours to prepare, but since several cameras were used—one of which was high-speed—it needed to be shot only once. "We didn't need more than about ten frames of the whole thing, but I wanted them to have a choice so they could use whichever footage came out the best. When we moved in with the syringe, we knew it was going to go very fast."

For Zoltan Elek and the alien-effects coordinators of Stan Winston Studios, *Alien Nation* proved to be one of the toughest films they had ever encountered. "I think we learned a lot about how difficult makeup shows really are," Shane Mahan muses. "The littlest thing can cause the biggest problem—the tiniest air bubble ruined everybody's night. We figured that going from something like the alien queen in *Aliens* to these straight prosthetic makeups would be simple, but it was really a lot of work. I hope people will understand we did our best under the circumstances. *Alien Nation* was a big show, and we did it in an incredibly short amount of time, thanks to a terrific crew that really worked well together." Despite the difficulties, Tom Woodruff found working on *Alien Nation* a nostalgic opportunity to pay homage to his career inspiration. "A number of us at the studio remember getting interested in makeup because of *Planet of the Apes*. It was one of the first big movies where most of the characters wore complete makeups. I personally got into makeup because of that movie, so to get the chance to do another big makeup picture like *Alien Nation* was great." The theme was a recurring one. "After *Pumpkinhead*, *Aliens*, and *Invaders from Mars*," concludes Alec Gillis, "we really wanted to do a straight prosthetic makeup show because we thought it would be so much simpler than all those mechanical heads we'd been making. Of course, the job we got was enormous—and presented its own unique problems that mechanical creatures do not have. The whole assembly-line process to create all the makeups we needed was a huge logistical challenge. At least it was nice to work on an effects show with some social significance."

This chapter on makeup was written by Ron Magid and originally appeared in Cinefex *magazine, #36.*

3 THE SERIES: AN INTRODUCTION

"We're like the cockroaches of science fiction," says actor Eric Pierpoint of *Alien Nation*. "You can try to stamp us out, but we keep coming back."

That's a pretty accurate observation, driven home by Fox Broadcasting which recently aired the fifth TV movie (*The Udara Legacy*, 1997) based on its short-lived 1989–90 TV series, having put into development a sixth (*City of Angels*), all of which followed on the heels of the high-rated *Dark Horizon* (1994), *Body & Soul* (1995), *Millennium*, and *The Enemy Within* (both 1996).

Shortly after its inception, Fox Broadcasting began looking for series properties that would differentiate the upstart network from the big three TV networks, and turned to its feature division for inspiration. One of the first titles that seemed a likely candidate was *Alien Nation*, the 1988 feature film that starred James Caan and Mandy Patinkin as human and Tenctonese cops Matthew Sykes (changed to Sikes for TV) and George Francisco. The challenge, naturally, was to find someone who could transform that theatrical release into a weekly series. The prime candidate was producer Kenneth Johnson.

Despite a variety of credits, including *The Bionic Woman* (1976–78), *The Incredible Hulk* (1978–82), and *"V"* (1984–85), Johnson was reluctant to jump into another TV series. "I'm really trying to steer away from episodic television, because it's rather like dropping yourself into a garbage disposal," he says matter-of-factly. "But Fox came to me, asking if I had seen their movie, which had opened very big."

He admits that he was impressed with the first half of the *Alien Nation* feature, but felt that the second half got lost in a typical crime plot line. He nonetheless loved the minority angle of the film's premise.

"I was very intrigued with the idea of exploring what it's like to be the latest people off the boat, as it were," he relates, "the newest addition to our society in America, and it's sort of an opportunity to explore what it was like to be the world's newest minority. At the same time we could explore what kind of cultural, ethnic, religious, mythological, biological differences these people represent. All of that was set up in the movie, but they didn't follow through on any of it. I suppose on the surface it's a buddy-cop show, but very quickly you realize that almost fifty percent of the show is devoted to what the guys' home life is like, and how the aliens are different from us and how the humans relate to them. It's really a show about cultural clash and cultural conflict. One new species trying to assimilate itself into another, which makes for a lot of conflict, a lot of anger, a lot of humor—'Welcome to Earth, here are your tax forms.'"

As an example, Johnson cites the fact that he decided it would take two male Newcomers to get one female pregnant, which raised more than a few eyebrows.

"The humans sort of look at it rather salaciously, until they come to understand that it's significant to these people. We wanted to, as best we could, mine the wealth of character material that you have when you have a new group of people trying to assimilate into another. It's rather like watching the Irish, the Jews, or the Italians coming to New York City in 1900, or watching the emergence of the black consciousness in the mid-'60s. Or the problems that the Vietnamese face today. When we were shooting the series, in northern California, a guy got shot just because he was Vietnamese. That's sort of what we were getting into on the show. It's not a sci-fi show in the sense that there are lasers, spaceships, and all of that sort of thing. It's really a character-based reality show that owes much more allegiance to *Cagney and Lacey* [1982–88] than *Miami Vice* [1984–89], *'V,'* or anything like that. These people are different. They have different physiologies, they have two hearts, they age at half the rate we do, they are a little keener with their senses than we are, they learn a little faster than we do...again, what I tried to do was make them all individuals. There are good Newcomers and evil Newcomers.

"It's a broad spectrum of society we were painting," adds Johnson, "with a good deal of humor, too. That's something very important to me, and it's something you obviously have when you're dropped into another country. You're dropped into France, you don't speak the language, and the jokes don't make sense to you. I think the pilot really speaks for itself. It's a strong piece of work. We had a sensational cast. There's not a weak performance between them, and the two key guys, Gary Graham and Eric Pierpoint, are really magical together, much as Jimmy Caan and Mandy Patinkin were in the film. We tried to take those two characters and these new actors made them their own, embraced them, and found new things to do as we went along."

During the course of the TV series, both Graham as Sikes and Pierpoint as Francisco attempted to explore the human condition by creating conflict with—and growing affection for—each other. It was that relationship that provided the heart and soul for the television series, and the chemistry between them is very similar to that which existed between William Shatner and Leonard Nimoy on the original *Star Trek* (1966–69).

"I'd like to think that I'm a good actor, and I know that Eric is wonderful," says Graham. "Boy, has he proven that to me. He's an incredible actor. And, yeah, people talk about chemistry. The first time we heard that was a few weeks into the filming of the pilot. They came back and said, 'This is great chemistry between the two of you.' And we said, 'Oh, really? What exactly do you mean?' You're used to hearing about chemistry between a male and female, the romantic relationship. I don't know what that is. All I know is that we listen to each other. For me, it's fairly easy. I look at that sponge-head and just react. It's kind of funny, and takes me off guard. His job is probably a lot more difficult, I'll admit that. It's just something that happens between two guys who feel comfortable doing what they're doing, which is the case with us. Plus we like each other as people, so it's a lot of fun to go to work, it's a lot of fun to make up things, and we check our egos at the door. He's got great ideas for my character, I've got good ideas for him. We just show up and try different things."

Pierpoint, who had previously worked with Johnson on the short-lived series *Hot Pursuit* (1984), shares Graham's enthusiasm about working together, pointing to an episode of the *Alien Nation* series called "Real Men" (TVS 17), which climaxes with George giving birth to a child and a bare-chested Sikes having to hug the infant close to him to keep it warm.

"I think when you look at something like that as an actor, you become fearful that you can't do what their image of it is; that it somehow comes off like a parody or you're making some kind of ridiculous anti-homophobic statement or something," he explains. "Gary and I had a lot of fun. We don't compete. We pretty much support each other, so it's a pretty unusual working relationship because this business can be so competitive. There are truly moments that if you just feel them, they'll come out right. I don't think we did much faking during the whole thing. I think that we genuinely like each other, so it's okay to do stuff like that. It's okay to say, 'Let's not care about being men for a second and see what happens.' It does get weird, but you see it and if it moves you when you're watching it, *that's* the most amazing thing. You sit there and say, 'Wow, I'm actually moved by this and it's on TV.' What a riot. That almost never happens."

In explaining the character setup in the series, Johnson notes that George is a bit of an "Uncle Tom," putting on human suits and ties, and trying to fit in, and going by the book. George's son, Buck, on the other hand, would rather speak their native language and hang out with his own kind, putting his father down for being a sellout to the humans. This conflict is further mirrored by the different viewpoints of the two leading characters, Matt Sikes and George Francisco.

"Yet they're both right," enthuses Johnson. "That, to me, is the essence of drama, where you can put two people in a room who are diametrically opposed and both are right. That gives you really good scenes, and that's sort of what we tried to do on the pilot and the series; to let Sikes articulate one point of view and George articulate another which is equally correct, but diametrically opposed. The sparks fly and the two actors are *so* good together. They support each other, love each other, and police each other all the time, and they developed a wonderful, sparky relationship that plays like gangbusters. The whole cast is great, and I'm grateful we had them."

In the *Alien Nation* feature film, Sykes was a bigot who, over the course of the film's running time, developed a solid relationship with George. On the series, Sikes could bounce back and forth between being a bigot and a liberal—an interesting dichotomy.

"What I wanted to show in Matt was that he was somebody who wore his prejudices right out there for everybody to see," says Graham, "but when it comes down to it, there's another side. His real nature is one of a very caring and involved human being. All this other bullshit just gets in the way. And, of course, the next day Matt would probably just reassemble his bullshit and kind of get back into being that macho guy. But when it comes right down to it, he does the right thing and he's a good, caring guy. What we've seen in the TV movies is Sikes going through a series of positive changes. He's learned to deal with his prejudices, learned more about the better side of humanity, and basically learned how to be a better human being. Being Joe Cynic may be integral to this character, but I don't see it as the whole ball of wax."

As for his relationship with George, he and Francisco are on a joint learning expedition, "teaching" each other about life.

"George is trying to teach me that it's okay to be as open and honest as he is; that innocence and optimism are essential in living a healthy life. Not a blind life, but a healthy life. He is much more of an optimist than I am. He is the gentle side of me, and it's okay to be as soft and as gentle as George can be. In fact, it's really kind of nice. But I think as we grow up as males, we feel as though we have to pretty much go out there and rope life into submission. We have to be aggressive, we have to be strong, we have to do all the outward things, and we harden ourselves a lot. He is the opposite of that. He's doing that, but not in the way that a human would."

"I try to put the most positive human traits in George and try not to give him the ones that will bring him down, which are the negative traits: selfishness, envy, jealousy, greed, cynicism," Pierpoint adds. "I'd rather have Sikes do it, because that's where you get the balance. George is learning a little bit more about real life from Sikes, but Sikes is learning much more about the inner man from George. That's the Yin-Yang going on in the show."

On his own, Eric nearly lost sight of the show's philosophy during the filming of the TV movie *Millennium* (1996), when, while waiting for an exterior setup to be arranged, a "gangbanger" approached, hit him in the head, and referred to him as a "cracker son-of-a-bitch."

"I damn near separated his head from his body," says Pierpoint, "because it was such an assault. The George philosophy didn't help me with this kid, which I guess is the difference between being George and being an actor. Later, though, the situation kicked me into another gear and I started to think, 'That kid actually gave me a gift that I forgot: This kind of situation is exactly what *Alien Nation* is about,' only it suddenly became very, very real."

For Johnson, *Alien Nation* as a weekly series and as TV movies represents further opportunities to deal not only with racial intolerance, but also his pet theme of humanism, which has shown up in many of his projects, including the TV series *The Incredible Hulk* (1978–82) and the theatrical release *Short Circuit 2* (1988).

"When I was in seventh grade, I chanced to see all of the film that was used in the Nuremberg Trials; all of the films of the death camps," he offers in explaining his thematic approach. "The piles of bodies, and the starved men, women, and children...it was really a turning point in my life. I was raised in sort of an anti-Semitic and bigoted household. My parents were from the South, although my father was [originally] from Massachusetts. Oddly enough, he was as much a bigot about black people as my mother was. They can't help it. They were raised that way. But something inside of me just instinctively knew that that was wrong.

"I happened to see those films because a friend of mine had a father in the Department of Defense, and he brought them into school one day for a group of seniors. It was only a handful of people that could see them. This was before you could see them on videotape, before they were generally available to the public. Never in my life had I even imagined anything like that, and when I saw it I was really so blown away that it caused me to re-evaluate my values and perceptions from early on. I couldn't deal with intolerance, I couldn't deal with bigotry. In some ways, a lot of my work has dealt with this."

He points to the feature film *Short Circuit 2,* which he considers to be another variation on the sensitive outsider portrayed in the film *The Elephant Man* (1980) or in the character of Quasimodo in Victor Hugo's novel *The Hunchback of Notre Dame* (1831) and its many screen adaptations. Looking at Johnny 5, the robot from that 1988 feature film, most people consider the "character" to be little more than nuts and bolts, and his big problem in the plot line was that nobody could appreciate the fact that he was alive; that there was a soul inside that robot.

"If you think about it," Johnson proposes, "he is exactly like the Elephant Man saying 'I am a human being.' That's what *Short Circuit 2* was really about for me; the struggle of this aberrant creature was to have people understand that he was alive, that he was a living, caring creature, and that's one of the big problems the Nazis had with the Jews. They would look at a person and see a stereotype or gender, as opposed to seeing an individual. The big hope I would have is that people come away from *Alien Nation* with the idea that you can't just look at somebody and categorically say, 'I don't like that person because they have no ears and no hair on their head.' You have to get to know them as a person before you make a value judgment of that kind. Of course, that's a metaphor or an allegory for a person that's black or a person that has almond eyes, or a person that is red-skinned, or a person who's white. I've felt it, too."

"Ever gone to Harlem by yourself?" Johnson asks rhetorically. "Do it. It's a strange experience, because all of a sudden you get it. A lot of people in motion pictures and television are Jewish, but I'm not. There are times when I've felt, 'How can I ever be successful in this business if I'm not Jewish?' It's a very strange feeling when all of a sudden you find that *you* have become the minority. That's part of what I wanted to touch on in the show; to raise people's consciousness a bit so that the next time they run into somebody who doesn't look like them or speak like them, they don't immediately type them or something worse."

This exploration would continue in future *Alien Nation* TV films, even though there was concern on the part of the studio about this format, as opposed to the one-hour series, as they felt that the two-hour telefeatures should be more "event"-driven.

"Kenny wants to veer away from going to outer space or saving the world in every film," says Graham. "The heart and soul of *Alien Nation* is the relationships. With the TV-movie format, you've got to make it big and expansive, but it really works, as he puts it, better in the framework of a [weekly] series where you can keep it all about relationships."

Pierpoint concurs, "Speaking with the network, it seems that they really do put pressure on us to develop larger-than-life story lines in the sense that there's got to be some big, overall event because they don't think they can sustain the movies with the characters. I'm pleased that *Millennium*, for instance, goes more into the character realm. There's more relationship going on in the Francisco family, more stuff going on between Matt and George, and more friction. That's the fun of *Alien Nation*, because if you lose that, you lose the show."

Johnson believes that, in the future, *Alien Nation* will continue to do what it does best, which is to "chip away" at the walls of prejudice, bigotry, sexism, racism, and intolerance of all sorts.

"I think if the '80s go down in history as the 'Me' decade, which seems to be the general consensus," Johnson offers, "all of us on *Alien Nation* are trying to bend our efforts toward making the '90s the 'We' decade. We hope we can accomplish at least a little bit of that, and keep chipping away at those walls."

During the course of the TV series, Johnson's creative collaborators included Andrew Schneider, Tom Chehak, Diane Frolov, Steven Mitchell, and Craig Van Sickle. These five names may not mean much to the general public, but they do, in fact, represent a part of the creative team that turned a mediocre motion picture into a television series that epitomized the word *quality*.

Bringing the Series to Life

Through its all-too-brief, one-season tenure on the Fox Broadcasting network, *Alien Nation* did what only a few movie-inspired TV series have been able to accomplish: it transcended its source material. Beyond the Service comedy *M*A*S*H* (1972–83) and Neil Simon's *The Odd Couple* (1970–75), it would be difficult to find another television series that has reached this creative goal.

What happened behind closed doors at Kenneth Johnson Productions during the 1989-90 television season was a bit of magic. These five writers, along with Johnson himself, conjured up a science-fiction TV series whose intelligence and insight into the human condition place it on a level with the classic *Star Trek*.

"Ken Johnson had very strong feelings about how the movie had gone wrong," says supervising producer Schneider. "It started with a very interesting premise of the latest wave of assimilating immigrants and then became this sort of cops-chase action picture. He really wanted to re-emphasize the racism metaphor that the movie started out with. That's sort of been our guiding premise. It's not so much a cop show as it is a show about racism and about people trying to assimilate into a culture.

"Also," Schneider continues, "the opportunity to spread this out over twenty-two episodes allowed us to continually explore new facets of their culture, physiology, and who they are. As in all good science fiction, it gave light to our own condition. In some ways it's more free than the cage of a two-hour movie. Diane [Frolov] and I are concerned that the shows we write have a very strong theme which is played out usually through several stories that have a thematic resonance. That's what made *Star Trek* so great. They were always dealing with major human themes in a science-fiction environment. That's what we've tried hard to do. We start with a premise which is fantastic and try to not go too much further out than our given premise. We try to keep a reality base in all of our episodes, not bringing in more people from outer space, or sea monsters. We try to adhere to the basic reality.

"Adding to the maintaining of that reality was the development of Sikes as well as George. Early on we saw the trap of just coming up with stories for the alien. If you do that, you're not servicing your human character. We tried very hard to give him [Sikes] texture, depth, and kind of a troubled past and things that play off against other aspects of these stories."

Co-producer Diane Frolov says, "Sikes is really us. He takes our place in the stories. Knowing about him and knowing about how he's reacting, always helps the story."

The fact that Sikes was a character in the throes of constant change was particularly pleasing to his real-life alter-ego. "One would think that it wouldn't be about evolvement, it would be about discovery," says costar Gary Graham. "Discovering the weirdness of the alien and the human's reaction to the alien. Our show is not so much about the aliens and it's not even that much of a cop show. It's relationships in evolution. That's always been our emphasis and the network fought us on that from the very beginning. From the outset Fox wanted a cop show. They wanted more car chases, bang-bang shoot-'em-ups, and had the attitude, 'There just aren't enough people dead.' Come on, give me a break. This show's about relationships and we always emphasized that. Toward the end of the first season, ironically, Fox came to Kenny and said, 'We want the scripts to have less cop stuff and more relationship stuff.' Kenny just looked at them and said, 'Okay, we'll have to do that.'"

Co-story editor Craig Van Sickle points out, "When you have a partnership show like this one, both have to be developed equally or it's lopsided. Obviously the initial temptation was to jump on George, because there was so much incredible stuff to do with his background. Meanwhile, you can't ignore the Sikes character. Initially, on the surface, he's just another TV cop we've seen before. But it had to be equal. It's easier to understand George through Sikes's eyes than it is to understand us through George's if it was a show just about an alien cop. By opening up viewers' eyes to who Sikes really was, it helped them to understand George's situation to a greater degree."

Tom Chehak, the co-producer, interjects, "It was a police detective show that could have an edge and actually say something, and not be the same run-of-the-mill police detective show. The idea was that we would delve into issues which other cop shows couldn't, and there was this whole alien side which was kind of interesting. So you could write a cop show, but also write a family show, and just about any story could work in there, depending on the issues we wanted to address. The cop arena just became a veneer for other things that were going on, which appealed to me."

4 TV SERIES EPISODE GUIDE

1989-90 Season

22 episodes, each 60 minutes
Originally aired on Fox Broadcasting
Based on characters created by Rockne S. O'Bannon

PRODUCTION CREW

Executive Producer:	Kenneth Johnson
Producer:	Arthur Seidel
Supervising Producer:	Andrew Schneider
Co-producers:	Diane Frolov, Tom Chehak
Associate Producer:	Mary Dick
Story Editors:	Steven Long Mitchell, Craig Van Sickle
Consultant:	Gale Anne Hurd
Unit Production Manager:	John Liberti
Directors:	(See Episode Credits for Director of Each Individual Episode)
1st Assistant Director:	Ken Stringer
2nd Assistant Director:	Alice Blanchard
Director of Photography:	Roland "Ozzie" Smith
Production Designer:	Ira Diamond
Editors:	Roosevelt Brody, David Strohmaier
Costume Designer, Men:	Jerry Herrin

Costume Designer, Women:	Diana Wilson
Original Music Score:	Steve Dorff, Larry Herbstritt
Music Theme:	Kenneth Johnson, David Kurtz
Casting:	Liberman/Hirschfield Casting, Irene Cagen
Script Supervisor:	Judi Brown
Set Decorator:	Sam Gross
Property Master:	Craig Binkley
Makeup Effects:	Rich Stratton
Special Effects Coordinator:	Burt Dalton
Stunt Coordinator:	Jon Epstein
Production Coordinator:	Katharine Reilly
Location Manager:	Edward Jeffers
Transportation Coordinator:	Dean Mason

REGULAR CAST

Gary Graham	(Matt Sikes)
Eric Pierpoint	(George Francisco)
Michele Scarabelli	(Susan Francisco)
Sean Six	(Buck Francisco)
Lauren Woodland	(Emily Francisco)
Terri Treas	(Cathy Frankel)
Jeff Marcus	(Albert Einstein)
Ron Fassler	(Captain Grazer)
Molly Morgan	(Jill) [Episodes 1-13]
Jeff Doucette	(Burns) [Episodes 1-13]
Lawrence-Hilton Jacobs	(Sergeant Dobbs) [Episodes 1-13]

AUTHOR'S EPISODE RATINGS

**** This Can't Be Television!

*** Damn, That Was Good

** You Can Do Better Than This, Guys

* Slag!

TVS 01. "ALIEN NATION"

Original Airdate: September 18, 1989
Writer: Kenneth Johnson
Director: Kenneth Johnson
Guest Cast: William Frankfather (Purist Leader)
Loyda Ramos (Puente)
Evan Kim (Dr. Lee)
Diane Civita (Jill's Mother)
Molly Morgan (Jill)

On their first assignment together, law enforcers Matt Sikes, an Earthling, and George Francisco, a Newcomer, investigate the bizarre death of a transient in Slagtown who developed an AIDS-like disease that quickly ravaged his body. In addition, there is a series of murders which seem to have been committed by a seven-foot-tall insect creature purported to have burst out of the skin of a Newcomer, a monster that seems to have ties with the human supremacist Purist movement.

At the same time, Sikes, who is still mourning the death of his human partner, William "Tuggs" Tuggle, is given a box of Tuggs's research regarding slavery and the aliens. He discovers a connection between his partner's death and the Overseers, those aliens who had reigned over the Newcomers on the slave ship and who now have made connections with many humans, including members of the police force.

NOTE: Newcomers, apparently, blink when they have a cold and express affection by touching each other's temples. Their form of sexual foreplay consists of humming over each other's back spots, and concentrated CO_2 (carbon dioxide) renders them unconscious. While humans' derogatory term for the aliens is Slags, they in turn refer to humans as Terts. The Newcomers' religious leaders are Andarko and Celine.

This episode also introduces the rest of the regular cast beyond Sikes and George, most notably Michele Scarabelli as George's wife, Susan Francisco; Sean Six as their son, Buck, and Lauren Woodland as their daughter, Emily; Terri Treas as Sikes's Tenctonese next-door neighbor, Cathy; Jeff Doucette as a tabloid reporter named Burns; and, in the police precinct, Lawrence-Hilton Jacobs (late of *Welcome Back, Kotter,* 1975-79, and assorted low-budget feature films) as Sergeant Dobbs; Jeff Marcus as Albert Einstein, the Newcomer janitor; and Ron Fassler as Captain Grazer.

Commentary

AUTHOR'S RATING: ***

What works against this pilot entry for the series are, in many ways, the same things that weakened the feature film, most notably the crime plot. Sikes and George's hunt for this supposed Tenctonese bug creature ultimately turns out to be a real distraction from what would eventually become the show's strong suit: its exploration of the culture clash between the Newcomers and humans in general, and the relationship between George and Sikes in particular. While the mystery is moderately intriguing, the bottom line is that this creature, at best, looks like a guy in a rubber suit. That that is what, ultimately, it is revealed to be doesn't diminish the fact that the obviousness of the disguise dissipates any real sense of jeopardy. Thus, the monster is not believably alien. An additional disappointment is that the accompanying AIDS allegory is introduced here, but not followed through in subsequent episodes of the series.

Despite these problems, what does work in this initial entry is its poignant exploration of racism, and how easy it is for some people to embrace their own. This is particularly powerful when you see blacks and, to a lesser degree, women appearing as fervent members of the Purists. Using the Francisco family as a prism in which these themes can be discussed works wonderfully, whether it be young Emily's dealing with life at a school in which she is the only Tenctonese student, or Buck's search for a direction to his young life. Ultimately, he joins a Newcomer gang, which, in turn, results in his shooting a human gang member during a skirmish. (Look for Tim Russ, later known as the Vulcan security chief on *Star Trek: Voyager* [1995–], who plays one of the human gang members.) Then, there is Susan, the concerned mother and wife, trying to make a new life for her family, and nearly forced back into a more sheltered existence due to the efforts of the Purists.

As intended, the real magic of *Alien Nation* is the relationship between Sikes and George. The creative spark between actors Gary Graham and Eric Pierpoint is immediate, echoing the power of William Shatner and Leonard Nimoy's first appearance together in the mid-1960's *Star Trek* pilot, "Where No Man Has Gone Before." As with Kirk and Spock, Sikes and George are two characters who essentially become whole when they're interacting together, and the show just isn't as interesting when they're not on screen at the same time.

Naturally there are some rough character edges in this pilot episode that, ultimately, would be smoothed out, though Pierpoint manages to convey an interesting Ghandi-like inner peace within George until the pressures of work and home become too much and the character explodes at his son, Buck, and at his cop partner, Sikes. The problem with Graham's onscreen alter ego in this TV pilot is that he and Ken Johnson have tried so hard to counter George's eternal optimism, that they have made Sikes too cynical for his (and our) own good. As a result, it's difficult for viewers to sympathize with him when he's so objectionable and argumentative with just about everyone he meets. However, there are a few oncamera moments when Matt's compassion shows through and the impression is given that this guy's bite somehow doesn't match up with his bark.

Behind-the-Scenes

Like most TV series pilots, *Alien Nation* introduced a variety of issues that provided the groundwork for many segments to come, though, in this case, some of them were ultimately discarded. Most notably, there is the plot line of the AIDS-like virus which Susan obviously has contracted at episode's end. Then, too, there is the whole script notion of Jill, the child who was going to be Emily's friend despite her mother's anti-Newcomer wishes. She is the one whom the mother planned to manipulate to harm the Francisco family, a move that goes for naught as the idea is dropped from the series altogether.

As supervising producer Andrew Schneider explains, "We had a feeling, all of us, when we came on staff, that it wasn't necessarily a good idea to continue the AIDS element. When you do a pilot, and Kenny created this huge tapestry, you have to go back and do the episodes and say, 'How can we clean this up now?' We were all kind of afraid that the AIDS story would take you down a path you've really kind of seen before, with someone with the disease really becoming a pariah and then the sadness of potential loss in the family. We all felt that it was such a downer and didn't really give us a lot of new stuff to explore, that we turned the disease into something which could come back, but might not."

"It really limited what we could do with the stories," points out co-producer Diane Frolov. "Obviously if you have one of your main characters dying, there's not a lot of room for levity. As far as Jill is concerned, it just happened that we had so many stories around, so much going on with the other characters, that we just couldn't find room for that story, so it kind of just disappeared."

"Plus," Schneider adds, "we didn't want to do a lot of stories about Purists and Purist conspiracies and that kind of thing. We did do those, but we were more interested in developing human interactions, humans dealing with the alien culture and vice-versa. We wanted to show the cultural differences rather than do conspiracy stories. It was not a real conscious effort to dump her, but in our priorities there didn't seem to be a lot of room for that."

One of Johnson's proudest creative moments comes when Purists protest Emily being in their kids' school, and Sikes finds himself defending her right to attend, essentially embarrassing the crowd into submission. After telling everyone they should be ashamed of themselves, it's capped off with Sikes looking at a black man and saying, "And you..."

"It's funny," Johnson explains, "because that's one of the things that the network wanted me to take out. I said, 'You sort of missed the point, guys.' Let me tell you something. I had finished shooting this pilot and we were in post-production, and somebody burned a cross five miles from my house in the San Fernando Valley—in 1989! *People* magazine did a short piece on us and gave us a 'B'. They said some pretty good things about it, but at one point they said the Purist thing was a little heavy-handed. Then they backed off from it. Look at the headlines, they said. Maybe it's not so heavy-handed; maybe it's what we need.

"My approach to the show," he elaborates, "is that it is essentially one species trying to assimilate into another, with all of the problems that that makes. There are some people who welcome them in, there are some bleeding-heart liberals who bend over backwards to welcome them in, and there are other people, like the Purists, who are sort of like the Ku Klux Klan. Instead of being white supremacist, they're human supremacist. They don't want the alien girl to go to their school. All of a sudden it looks like Mississippi in 1965, and it's the opportunity to sort of look at our society through that prism. To have a minority that nobody has an investment in here, so we're not offending anyone, but we can discuss what it's like to be different, what it's like to have a different racial background, what it's like to have different-colored skin or a different-shaped head, and what it's like to try to blend in. That leads into all kinds of wonderful scenes of drama and conflict and humor."

Most significant about the pilot, naturally, was the casting of Gary Graham as Matt Sikes and Eric Pierpoint as George Francisco, the duo who would ultimately represent the heart and soul of the series, and both actors instinctively knew that these were the roles of a lifetime.

For Graham, much of his preparation for the role of Sikes came from spending time with one of his best friends, T. J. Hageboeck, a sergeant headquartered at the Los Angeles Sheriff's office.

"I went on drive-alongs, went to cop bars, and hung out and listened to cop stories," he reflects. "From the get-go, T. J. would introduce me to his cop friends, judges, bartenders—everybody—as his partner, Gary. They just shook my hand and assumed I was carrying a piece and wearing a badge, like I was working undercover or something. He never said anything different, so everybody treated me as if I was a copper. I was privy to some pretty interesting conversations being 'one of them'—none of which I would repeat. Man, I really got a crash course in what it feels like."

Also providing an influence for Graham was James Caan's portrayal of the same character in the 1988 feature film.

"When I was cast, I had not seen the original movie, and Ken Johnson said, 'You might want to take a look at it,' so I saw it the night before we started work. It must have colored me subliminally. There was a lot of stuff that I liked in James Caan's portrayal, and a lot of stuff I didn't care for. Ultimately, I think I'm glad that I did watch it, because just before we took off with filming I think I made a small adjustment and I gave Sikes perhaps a little tougher edge than I would have. Just influenced by Caan's performance. Not to say that I stole anything, but subliminally I said, 'Yeah, I'm going to borrow just a shred of that and color it with the way I've been approaching it,' and that's what I came up with. I like that balance, that kind of sarcastic smart-ass who's also playful. Although not as angry as Caan's take on the character, I decided that Sikes was the kind of guy who wakes up on the wrong side of the bed every morning."

For his part, costar Eric Pierpoint looks back warmly at the shooting of the pilot, noting that he, too, was somewhat influenced by his predecessor in the role, Mandy Patinkin.

"The part of the film that worked was mainly the first half of the movie where Mandy and James Caan were settling into who they were," says Pierpoint. "That was the most fun for me. Mandy, the way he did it, gave George a certain steadiness, a certain kind of stalwart reliability and openness that I thought was really keepable, as well as a kind of tongue-in-cheek sense of humor. That's consistent with what Ken Johnson and I were thinking. From there you've got a lot more leeway, because if it goes to series you can start taking all kinds of chances and take it in other directions. But it was fun because it was a real camaraderie, a real 'getting to know you' project with all of the actors."

Pierpoint views the pilot as a time of great, terrifying, on-the-set discovery, as relationships both in front of and behind the camera began to jell.

"When I look back at the pilot," he muses, "I think, 'This was the beginning and I could see how I took this and ran with it later on, and how I discarded that.' You're really kind of feeling your way around, especially with a character that you're not sure how complicated he really is or how complicated he can get. When you see most pilots, oftentimes you'll see in the ensuing series that certain characters are feeling their way and won't hit their stride for about six episodes. Some people actually nail it right on and don't change. Some you throw against the wall and whatever sticks, you keep. Then you make adjustments, refine it, and make it, hopefully, better.

"The pilot was a wonderful adventure because everything was new," continues Pierpoint. "The makeup was new, the characters were new. It was sort of like the first couple of weeks of rehearsal on a play where you're trying stuff out and it's very creatively pure because you don't have anything in the bag, so you're trying to be as true as possible to what you need to do to make sense out of it. You also have to define what you feel are going to be the qualities which are best going to suit this character."

Enjoyable to the actor was the initial sense of self-contained distance between him and Gary Graham, which played out so well between George and Sikes. "There's more of a sense of territory around each character in the pilot as we're feeling our way around," he says. "I really like that because it seemed totally appropriate for what would have happened in real life. And we didn't know each other's strengths and weaknesses as actors. When I saw the pilot later, it seemed very real to me. We're not a comedy team—yet! Later you become more familiar and there's a new character going on, which is the Matt-and-George character. It's like a married couple. When they meet they are each their own person, but when they're together they create a new element or person."

Incidentally, if one looks closely at the action during much of the pilot, one will notice that Gary Graham is actually limping. A week into filming, the actor tore his Achilles tendon, but due to time constraints he was not able to tend to it properly before resuming shooting. "It required surgery and about six weeks in a full leg cast," he laughs, "and we were barely into production and I couldn't go in for surgery for another three and a half weeks. I gave it a good athletic wrap, did some hobbling, and they did some skillful cutting around it. So that was really on my mind. A lot of the pilot was pain and me wondering how I was going to be able to do it."

TVS 02. "FOUNTAIN OF YOUTH"

Original Airdate: September 25, 1989
Writer: Diane Frolov
Director: John McPherson
Guest Cast: Jason Beghe (Trenner)
Joel Polis (Windsor)
Steve Rankin (Henry James)
Gretchen Graham (Lisa)
Susan Gibney (Harriet Beecher)
James Greene (Uncle Moodri)

While saving George, Newcomer police officer Henry James is shot in the arm by a suspect, and is brought to a Tenctonese clinic. A human doctor in residence (Jim Trenner) turns out to be a former teenage crony of Sikes's and the two men share a joyful reunion.

The next day, George attempts to visit Officer James and is told that he died of respiratory failure during surgery. Naturally, George is shocked, and unable to accept the situation, and begins a private investigation, ultimately learning that several other Newcomers have recently died at the clinic from the same cause and that a gland that controls their metabolism was removed from each victim. Eventually, he and Sikes discover that Trenner, who is actually a Purist, has been killing patients for this gland, which is being used to control the aging of humans.

NOTE: We learn that Newcomers have pink blood, refer to themselves as the Tenctonese, and that, following adolescence, their growth rate slows down to such a degree that George is actually seventy solar years to Sikes's thirty-five, and that the average Newcomer life-expectancy is 140.

Also to be noted is that most Newcomers have taken on names of famous Earth people (such as the writer Henry James in this episode and various Earth film stars, scientists, and so forth, in subsequent episodes), or objects. This appropriation of real (or sometimes fictitious) human names or appellations often lead to ironic conclusions about the character of the individual Newcomer within the script plot.

Commentary

AUTHOR'S RATING: ***½

Some great comic possibilities are explored during a precinct basketball game in which Sikes and George are assigned to the same team. George's on-the-court movements are hysterical, and it's a scene that easily could have been featured in the acclaimed TV series *The Odd Couple* (1970–75), and, indeed, might very well have been. Additional humorous moments are explored when Sikes pulls a groin muscle during the game, and he finds himself constantly being looked at or questioned by George and his neighbor Cathy.

For much of the episode, Sikes comes across as a bigot, particularly in his attempts to tell a "sponge-head" joke. His perception changes ever so slightly when he attends a party hosted by Trenner and he overhears somebody else telling the same joke. Graham has a nice reaction to this, given the opportunity to essentially eavesdrop on himself. Another nice touch is seen when Sikes stocks sour milk in the cupboard for George in case he comes by to visit.

Guest star Jason Beghe is sufficiently smarmy and arrogant as Dr. Trenner, and it's difficult not to take an instant dislike to this character. For his part, Eric Pierpoint's big moment in the episode comes when he is successfully able to display his simmering rage—and horror—at watching a Trenner videotape in which his friend Officer James is essentially murdered on the operating table.

There's a wonderful final moment when George tries to stop Sikes from destroying Trenner's research, believing that it could, in the right hands, be used for good. "That's what they said when they split the atom," sneers Sikes. "*Never* bet on the goodness of the human race." A sad, but true fact that gives the end of the episode a particular moral tone.

Behind-the-Scenes

"Fountain of Youth" was the third episode shot, but the first to air following the series' pilot.

Co-producer Diane Frolov, who had previously collaborated with Johnson on the first draft of "*V*"-*The Final Battle* (1984) and *Shadow Chasers* (1985–86), says, "What we wanted to do there was deal with the human attitude about aging. We started with a little story about how Susan is trying to get a job and finds that she's too old for the job market. In the end, she ends up lying about her age in order to get a job. We also played a thing between Sikes and George where we learned that the aliens age at a much slower rate than humans, so they're actually much older than they seem. Sikes is turning thirty-seven [*sic*], and is depressed about it. All of that gave us the character material that we needed."

Supervising producer Andrew Schneider notes, "That episode was made at a time when a lot of people had their fingers in the pie. Also, any show needs a kind of start-up time usually to hit its stride. I think that generally the second half of the season was stronger as we evolved how we wanted to do the show."

"That was a pretty effective idea, with a nice science-fiction backdrop to it," notes Craig Van Sickle, "and a good way to kick the show off in terms of what the aliens mean to society."

Co-story editor Steven Mitchell adds, "It also allowed us to not only look at the emotional and physical impact of the Newcomers, but also a biological one. The first three episodes were spent pretty much feeling the show out and figuring out exactly what it was."

Co-producer Tom Chehak believes that they *had* to do a show along these thematic lines. "It was the obvious show where you kill an alien to benefit the greed of the human condition," he says. "Like you would take from an animal and use it on a person. What price youth? What price life? A pretty obvious show, and not that special to me."

Gary Graham felt a certain affinity to Sikes's feelings in this episode at the time, though since becoming a father he admits that things have grown considerably brighter. "I'm over forty, so I've confronted the 'gee, I'm getting older and it takes longer to heal' syndrome," he says. "'Gee, is that more gray hair?' But then you have a daughter and who cares? I feel younger today than I did years ago. 'Fountain of Youth,' though, is pretty powerful stuff. I think it's the ultimate insult using these people as organ donors, with the plan probably being to breed them for that purpose. It was a pretty frightening show in that regard."

Eric Pierpoint adds, "Newcomers being served up almost as spare parts to keep the humans rolling along—that's very interesting because [Louis] Farrakhan came out with something that said blacks are being killed off or used as body parts for whites. Interesting, we dealt with that plot years ago."

For the actor, the episode featured several highlights, most of them humorous. "How does George play basketball?" he asks rhetorically. "He gets a little confused and combines what he thinks football is and basketball. He's got his arm stretched out straight and is dribbling, being guarded by this very athletic woman. Instead of passing the ball to Matt, he just kind of takes an eye on the basket and throws a hook shot from about thirty feet. I'm telling you, one take and it went in, so we didn't have to do a follow-up shot of the ball going in. We all rushed toward the basket and were trying to get through the scene without falling on the ground laughing hysterically, because the whole crew started to laugh during this. It was such a George thing to do—out of nowhere he throws a hook shot and it just happens to go in. We got through the scene, they called 'cut' and everybody just falls on the ground laughing. I said to the director, 'I just saved you about twenty grand of new setups in having to cover this.' They got it in one!

"Then," he adds, "we take on the scene where Matt pulls a groin muscle and we get into what I consider some very funny opportunities—which is Matt and George sitting on the couch, finding out more about each other. Sitting on the couch and he's putting an ice pack on his crotch and George is watching, curious, just staring at it with all the calm and ease of, 'That's interesting.' Matt is like, 'What are you looking at?' He's sitting next to this alien who's looking at his crotch, and then they get into a discussion about age and he finds out that George is in his seventies, which bowls him over. You find out mainly that George is middle-aged and that aliens live about twice as long as humans. I found that to be a really well-written, good scene—a combination of comedy and fact played out with the characters, and making it that third entity I've talked about before."

TVS 03. "LITTLE LAMB LOST"

Original Airdate: October 2, 1989
Writer: Diane Frolov
Director: Kevin Hooks
Guest Cast: James Greene (Uncle Moodri)
Heather McAdam (Mary Shelley)
Shannon Wilcox (Charlotte Bronte)
Kimberly Kates (Dallas)
Will Bledsoe (Dorian Grey)
William Wellman Jr. (Rudy)
Trevor Edmond (Blentu)
Noon Orsati (Svabo)
Catherine Lansing (Receptionist)

Sikes and George try to save Tenctonese prostitute Mary Shelley, but she is killed by Dorian Grey, henchman of the girl's pimp. Looking into her past, the intrepid cops trace both Mary and Dorian to a talent agency operated by Newcomer Charlotte Bronte, who turns out to be an Overseer still controlling her former slaves (this time making them prostitutes) and making a hefty living for herself on Earth.

A subplot involves George's uncle, Moodri, and the man's devotion to Tenctonese religion touching the soul of Buck, who comes forward to the police and confesses to the accidental shooting of the black gang member, which occurred in the pilot episode.

NOTE: Whereas humans get sore necks as a result of tension, the Tenctonese suffer from sore feet.

Commentary

AUTHOR'S RATING: **½

The Purists spend a great deal of their time proclaiming what a corruptive influence the Tenctonese are on our society, but they fail to note humanity's impact on the Newcomers, introducing them to all kinds of previously unexplored vices, such as drugs and prostitution.

This episode effectively chips away at Sikes's cynicism. Mary reminds him somewhat of his own teenage daughter and, as a result, his basic humanity begins to emerge. Ironically, it seems that the Newcomers are having more of a psychological impact on him than his fellow humans.

Some surprising poignancy comes from George's Uncle Moodri, when he reaches out to Buck who's still reeling mentally from the shooting of the gang member, Campbell. Moodri proves to the youth that faith plus belief in the notion that we are all part of the same universe is what's needed to survive. Sean Six's Buck undergoes some intriguing self-exploration here, thanks largely to his disillusionment with his gang, when he realizes that all they care about is having sex and creating havoc. There is no desire on their part to maintain the old way of Tenctonese life, and as far as he's concerned they're as corrupt as the Terts. The episode surely marks Six's best performance on this TV series.

Behind-the-Scenes

Ken Johnson admits to being intrigued by the notion of our influence on the Tenctonese. "In a slave society," he muses, "prostitution has no value, because you can't own anything. All of a sudden you're in a free society and it's great, but then new pressures come to bear and your body has value. As well as a liberating influence we've had on these aliens, we've had a corrupting influence on them."

"The initial idea," recalls Diane Frolov, "came from the film *The Emerald Forest* [1985]. We wanted to examine an innocent in the wild and the idea that these creatures didn't have any idea about prostitution before they came here. It was an influence of Earth."

"Their sexuality was different," offers Andrew Schneider, producer of *The Incredible Hulk* (1978–82) and *Northern Exposure* (1990–96). "They didn't have sex with someone they weren't intimate with emotionally, so for them it was a very foreign concept. We wanted to examine the way that humanity casually accepts prostitution as a part of human nature."

Tom Chehak and Craig Van Sickle of the *Alien Nation* production team didn't share their enthusiasm. "Didn't work," Chehak shrugs. "I felt it was a badly constructed episode. The message was right, but I didn't feel that we got the emotional involvement that we needed from our main characters. I should preface this by saying that there were some really strong moments, but it wasn't a great show."

Van Sickle interjects, "That show probably least represented what we wanted to do with the series. On the one hand, it dealt with the social ramifications of how they came into our lives and started doing things that certain humans did. It was a good episode to show that side of it, but it was one of those episodes that kind of got caught in the feeling-out of the series and trying to figure out what would work for the show. Inevitably in any TV season, you're going to have a few episodes that struggle a little bit more, if you will, in finding the proper 'voice.'"

During production, co-lead Gary Graham felt a kinship with guest star Heather McAdam, who portrayed Mary. "Heather felt like my little sister or daughter," he recalls. "I feel such empathy for kids anyway and one of the most touching moments of the episode was when I say to her, 'Why don't you take off?' and she says, 'I have nowhere to go.' A lot of kids, especially in Los Angeles, are like that. They have no place to go or they *feel* as if they have no place to go. It's such a tragedy that you just want to scoop them up and take them all home, but then they'd probably rob you or something. My former church, Hollywood Presbyterian, has a place on Hollywood Boulevard to take in runaways and administer to them. I used to contribute to that. It's a big problem, kids who are just confronted with homelessness. They don't think that anybody loves them or cares about them, or their parents never conveyed their feelings. I think this was an *important* episode for us to do."

Eric Pierpoint adds, "I would think that Newcomers suffer from the typical cultural disease, the easy buck. . . . I think the important thing to know from my perspective is that just because they're Newcomers doesn't mean they have any greater capacity, as a race, for morals or for accomplishments. It's all the same. You take people race by race, no matter what race it is, and you're going to have people abused by the system or people abusing the system. I think that's the important thing. . . ."

"I remember a scene," Pierpoint continues, "where one of the prostitutes is set up with a wire, and George goes in at the end and embraces her in a very fatherly, compassionate way, and understands how hard it is for these young people to make it in the world. Can you imagine being transported to another planet as a human and really having nothing to offer but your sexuality? That would be kind of mind-blowing, especially to a race that you didn't find particularly attractive and are just being picked clean by perverts or curiosity seekers. It makes you wonder about the kids wandering the streets now, thinking that their only worth is their sexuality, that they are some kind of instrument or commodity to be used for a few bucks. They have nothing else to offer. It's a sad state of affairs."

TVS 04. "FIFTEEN WITH WANDA"

Original Airdate: October 9, 1989
Writers: Steven Long Mitchell and
Craig Van Sickle
Director: Rob Bowman
Guest Cast: David Bowe (Buster Keaton)
Lori Petty (Sal)
Joan McMurtrey (Victoria Fletcher)
Cheryl Pollak (Kirby Sikes)
Wayne Pere (Thor)
Sachi Parker (Wanda)
Bobbie Cummings (Ernie Jett)
Trevor Edmond (Blentu)
Noon Orsati (Svabo)
Jean Sincere (Granny)
Ron Howard George (Wayne Joshua)

This episode examines parenting from a variety of angles: Sikes is having a difficult time with his daughter, Kirby, who only contacts him when she wants something, and manipulates him in any way she can; and George tries to cope with the rebellious spirit of Buck, who is still getting into fights with human students at school while trying also to remove himself from his former gang.

All of this occurs while the detectives guard a Newcomer named Buster Keaton, who is scheduled to testify against a murdering mobster. The situation is complicated by Buster's hormonal need to be with his girlfriend, Wanda, and the arrival of hitman Ernie Jett, who will stop at nothing to silence Keaton.

NOTE: Besides meeting Sikes's daughter, Kirby, we also encounter his ex-wife, Virginia, who could not tolerate being wed to a cop who is so married to his job. On the Newcomer front, we learn that the Tenctonese were never allowed to be parents, as they were separated from their offspring by the Overseers when the children were only ten years old.

Commentary

AUTHOR'S RATING: **½

If there were any doubts of *The Odd Couple*'s influence on *Alien Nation*, one does not have to look any further than this installment. George is the quintessential, gruff, sloppy Oscar Madison, and Sikes is his nemesis, overly-fastidious Felix Unger.

Where this episode blossoms is in its examination of the pressures of parenting. Sikes has been an absentee father for the past eighteen years and now has to deal with a manipulative daughter. The relationship is at a crucial crossroads and Graham is terrific as a father desperately trying to mend fences before it's too late.

George's plight with Buck is just as problematic. We learn that, at age ten, children were taken from their parents on the slave ship and that the "freedom" afforded the Tenctonese on Earth has done little to rectify parent-offspring relations while the pressures of their "new" life keep ripping them apart. Pierpoint, too, successfully conveys his character's pain and desperation to make things right without really knowing how to do so. Michele Scarabelli's Susan Francisco takes a parenting lesson from an episode of the TV show *Bonanza* (1958–73), and is hysterically funny in her application of it to her family.

Where the episode falls flat is in its clumsy handling of the action sequences. These are *really* disappointing, particularly a shootout at a lingerie shop which is ineptly staged and badly edited. Then, too, when Buck attempts to excise himself from his gang and is beaten up as a result, Susan's rescue of her son is ludicrously dramatized: the gangbangers just stand patiently by so she can kick each of them savagely in turn.

As a character study, this episode is wonderful. However, just try to forget the action bits.

Behind-the-Scenes

"Of all the shows we wrote, this was probably the least strong," admits story editor Steven Mitchell, who, along with his co-story editor, Craig Van Sickle, is co-creator of NBC's *The Pretender* (1996–). "It was kind of like *thirtysomething* [1987–91], where the whole show dealt with their relationships, their children, their parenthood. While the script was pretty good, it could have moved a bit faster."

"There were some levels in the script that didn't quite make it to the screen," offers Van Sickle. "Part of it is because it's one of the first episodes that was shot. Everybody was still kind of getting the rhythms down and feeling everybody out. That was a show, had we done it in the back nine, would have come out much better, because Gary and Eric would have known their rhythms with each other a little more, and the audience would have been able to 'give' more of themselves to what was going on. They would have understood the character nuances. This was an important episode in the eventual evolution, in that it really did focus on our two guys. There was no case at all. Actually, it was one of the few episodes in the whole season where there was no case."

Mitchell says, "Sometimes, as writers and producers, you forget that you've been sitting in a room for six months, talking about these characters. We know them very well, but the audience who is watching this show has only visited with them a couple of times, so they are not as aware of them. As episode three is being shown to the audience, we're already working on episodes ten, eleven, and twelve, so we've spent so much more time with them that there's a natural evolution of the characters. Success in this medium almost predicates itself on your audience knowing your characters. Then, when they're in a situation like a prostitution ring or the situations of many of the later episodes, once you know that character, you know how they're going to react. You understand what's not being written or said, because you already care for that character. It's been our experience that once you know the characters, it helps the show later on. I think once people have seen all the episodes and then go back to that one, they're going to know George and Sikes fairly well. You go back to it and put more in that might not have been there the first time."

Offers co-producer Tom Chehak, "The studio wanted a humorous show. There are two shows that are very typical of writing what the network or studio wanted. That was 'Takeover' [TVS 05] and 'Fifteen with Wanda.' This was written to be a comedy and 'Takeover' was written as hard action.

That's what the battle was. What are we doing here, action drama or comedy? I think both of them have a little bit of merit, but not a lot. Obviously we created a couple of characters that we dealt with, and it was a good show up front to explore a lot of alienness."

Rob Bowman, a producer-director of *The X-Files* (1993–) and director of the feature film (1998) based on that TV series, helmed this particular episode. Bowman is the son of veteran director Chuck Bowman, and his style here tremendously impressed Gary Graham. "I liked him," he laughs. "He drove a lot of the guys crazy, but I thought he was great. He was very innovative, being fresh to the business, which allowed more experimenting with us. In fact, there were a couple of moments when we were in the motel with that guy that just cracked me up. I made myself laugh a couple of times, although that's generally not acknowledged as one of our better episodes. I'm sort of critical of myself in all of my scenes. I could have done more or maybe waited until I was a real father."

"An interesting show," adds Eric Pierpoint, "because it was such a claustrophobic feeling sitting there in that motel room. I really do think there are times when Matt and George are like Felix and Oscar. I look at something like 'Fifteen with Wanda' as being a Felix-and-Oscar kind of thing, where Matt is even more of a slob and George becomes even more anal, constantly tidying things up. He's really at his wits' end because the humans are stinking more and more, and he's got no relief at all and is ready to explode. I look at that situation as an attempt at finding all of the elements of drama and comedy in a hotel room. I figure if you're going to steal, then you have to steal from the best, and *The Odd Couple* is a classic. Neil Simon created a situation that's very, very classic.... Doing 'Fifteen with Wanda' [proved to be] a dance in comic frustration.... Matt is the roommate that most people could not abide—actually, they're both roommates people could not abide. One who makes these time demands on you and makes you clean up after your bread crumbs, and the other one who is a complete slob. Put them together and it's hell. Funny, but hell."

TVS 05. "THE TAKEOVER"

Original Airdate: October 16, 1989
Writer: Tom Chehak
Director: Steve Dubin
Guest Cast: Charley Lang (Kenny Dunstan)
Ji-Tu Cumbuka (Andrew Craig)
Gwynyth Walsh (Diane Elrea)
Tracey Walter (Tom Mulden)

Due to a series of riots throughout Los Angeles, George and Sikes are the only ones left in the precinct to answer calls, dispatch cops, and so forth. As Susan visits the precinct, bringing George his lunch and retrieving his dirty uniform to be cleaned, a truck pulls up outside with a group of male humans and a female Newcomer, who are planning to rob the valuable contraband being held as evidence within the now near-empty precinct.

Sikes is called out on an emergency, and the gang moves in, taking Susan hostage and stealing over $10 million in drugs, as well as a canister of gas used by the Overseers to control the slaves aboard the ship. The Tenctonese female thief has found that the gas works on humans as well, and hopes to take over the planet with its use.

NOTE: In this episode human body-odor in close proximity results in irritability in Newcomers.

Commentary

AUTHOR'S RATING: *½

This episode proves to be, easily, the worst of the *Alien Nation* series. Its design was obviously two-fold: to appeal to the action fan and to cash in on the success of the original *Die Hard* film (1988), in the sense of having a lone cop (George Francisco) in a confined space (the police station) trying to take down the bad guys while simultaneously trying to save his wife (Susan).

The premise works fine if your lead is Bruce Willis and you have a multi-million-dollar budget at your disposal, but *Alien Nation* has neither. As a result, the episode is an aberration within the body of the TV series. This is *not* an action show, and any straying from the elements that truly make the series work invariably fails. Even the comic relief of having Captain Grazer attending a conference on the riot, armed with his college thesis, falls flat. In fact, this installment is so sloppy that there isn't even internal story-line continuity. At one point, one of the bad guys announces that he's leaving, but, later, he's shown involved in a shootout with Sikes and Dobbs who have come to back up George.

The one part of the episode that does work is the exploration—and ultimate criminal value—of the gas used on the slave ship by the Overseers to keep the Tenctonese docile. An episode devoted to the impact of that gas would have been preferable to this mishmash.

Behind-the-Scenes

"The network decided they wanted a harder-action show, a more traditional cop show," explains supervising producer Andrew Schneider. "That was written by Tom Chehak, and I think it was successful for what it was, but in terms of the show that we later evolved, it really isn't thematically what we wanted to do. It doesn't deal with the big themes, the human-alien interaction we prefer to do. Particularly the science-fiction fans like the kind of show that we tried to do more of, which deals with a metaphor for our own condition. A show like 'Takeover' doesn't really give you that."

Tom Chehak agrees. "Nothing," he says matter-of-factly. "Just one of those bare-shelled scripts. I think basically what went wrong is that it was a show that didn't really have an alien hook other than the gas. It could have been an episode of *Hunter* [1984–91]. It was incongruous with the rest of the series, but if you want action, there it is."

"An episode that was done at the request of the studio," says co-story editor Steven Mitchell. "They wanted a real action show. The nice thing about *Alien Nation* is that if you look at the first three to five episodes, they were almost all distinctly different. They were real diverse, distinct personalities in terms of episodes. Again, I think that was something we needed to do, exploring different aspects of the relationships. 'Takeover' was hard action, but we were able to give it an alien twist with the gas, which told us more about the Newcomers. One of the beauties of the show was that you could take what on the surface appears to be a standard cop plot, and make it something much more than that.

"'Takeover' was almost an episode of *S.W.A.T.* [1975–76] with bald people," he smiles. "When we did that, I think we found that's not where the money was with this show, which is why we didn't do future episodes like it. It's one of those things where it's nice to have the opportunity to take a chance and see if it works. If you look at something like *Star Trek*, the episodes where it's just a space battle, with a lot of phasers and torpedoes firing, are not as exciting as Spock and Captain Kirk on a planet where they may live or die. We were sort of glad to take that chance, but overall it was probably not indicative of what the show was about."

Eric Pierpoint refers to "Takeover" as the "Bruce Willis" episode, representative of a committee-type situation that occasionally existed during the run of the series. "Sometimes you've got a lot of people coming in and trying different kinds of scripts to see what works. You take Matt and George and put them in a hotel room or you put them on a baseball field. You just do different things with them. This one was supposed to be an intense-action kind of gritty film. It's a lot less complicated. There's mainly one thing going on, and you've got George basically trying to track down the bad guys by himself with a big gun. I don't remember it as being a particularly satisfying episode to do. It's not a real *Alien Nation* script. The heart of *Alien Nation* is in the by-play between aliens and humans and the inner workings of Matt and George; how Matt is doing with Cathy and how Matt is doing with the Francisco family. You've got to bring him in and out of that situation to hit all the strides of the show and get Matt and George working on each other so that they reveal the world through their eyes together. 'Takeover' is not that kind of show, unfortunately."

For actor Gary Graham, "Takeover" was a reunion of sorts with veteran performer Tracey Walter, who had appeared in one of the actor's early films, *Hardcore* (1979). "We were reminiscing," says Graham, "and he said, 'Now you've got this series going for you,' and I said, 'Yeah, we're having a great time, it's enjoyable.' He responded, 'Forget about that. The main thing is you get all that cash. Just get that cash.' I thought that was great. For my part, though, the episode was the worst one I'd ever done just because we had two days on this location, on something that used to be a toxic waste dump. It was this horrible, horrible industrial sight and everywhere you turned there were warnings, 'Stay Away, Do Not Breathe.' What the hell were we doing there? We all kind of cut it short a little bit and got out of there. I think we were supposed to be there for four days, but we got out in two. Just this horrible, horrible place. That was my recollection—an episode you wanted to leave."

TVS 06. "THE FIRST CIGAR"

Original Airdate: October 23, 1989
Writers: Diane Frolov and Andrew Schneider
Director: John McPherson
Guest Cast: James Greene (Uncle Moodri)
Cary-Hiroyuki Tagawa (Yamato)
Joon B. Kim (Korean)
Diana Bellamy (Betsy Ross)
Steve Susskind (Vahan)
John Patrick Reger (Ramna)
Trevor Edmond (Blentu)
Noon Orsati (Svabo)
Carolyn Mignini (Ruth Steelman)

Struggling to pay a debt of $2,400 to the IRS, George finds himself having to go to successful Newcomer businesswoman Betsy Ross for a loan. Ross, who claims to be impressed with the progress that George, one of their own, has made on this planet, is happy to help, and, in addition, insists she can get for him information about dealers of the highly-addictive narcotic "Jack," termed "the crack of the '90s."

Sikes doesn't trust Ross, but George refuses to accept his argument until it becomes clear that Ross is actually an Overseer trying to corner the Jack market for herself.

NOTE: This was to be the first regular series episode, but it was delayed until this point, thus the inclusion of awkwardness between George and Sikes as new partners. "The First Cigar" also hinted toward a possible romantic connection between Sikes and Cathy.

Commentary

AUTHOR'S RATING: ***

The episode provides a few intriguing character studies. Buck, the proverbial alien-without-a-cause, gets sucked into a real estate scheme as a salesman and becomes so blinded by the lure of the money that he turns into the same type of "sell-out" that he constantly accuses his father of becoming. His disillusionment when he realizes he's been taken is palpable, and you can see why he remains a lost soul, torn between his heritage as a Tenctonese and life on Earth. Not trusting humans, he has been betrayed first by his former gang and, now, by con man Sam Simian.

George's confrontation with the IRS is a humorous sketch, particularly his mistaken pride as a former slave standing up for himself and refusing to pay, and Sikes's suggestion that he grovel for forgiveness.

The real heart of the episode is Diana Bellamy's Betsy Ross, apparently a successful Tenctonese businesswoman who is actually an Overseer. Bellamy brings such a presence to her role that Ross emerges as one of the most ruthless and powerful Overseers seen on this series. Pierpoint does a nice job of portraying George's initial reluctance to accept gifts from Ross, his later rationalization when she loans him the money needed to pay his tax bill, and his chagrined realization that, unknowingly, he's been working with an Overseer.

This episode also represents the first emotional "moment" between Sikes and Cathy. It begins with a plumbing problem and ends with them exchanging wine and sour milk—you get the sense that there's *something* romantic developing between the two of them.

Director John McPherson handles the proceedings well, establishing nice suspense in an early scene involving a drug bust. Outstanding is the final shootout where, right in the midst of the heavy-duty action, there's humorous banter between Sikes and George that mirrors similar moments between Kirk and Spock on TV's original *Star Trek*.

Behind-the-Scenes

"It was about corruption and how one can be seduced very easily if one is not careful," says co-producer Diane Frolov. "Originally it was supposed to be our first episode, and at the time we were trying to tie up so many stories, there were so many people involved in that episode, and we were trying to set up the world we lived in in 1995. We were trying to do many, many things in that episode and it all kind of got scattered. The resolution of the Buck story was originally in that one, and we moved it completely. We had to substitute another Buck story, where he was involved with this guy who was selling real estate."

Andrew Schneider, the supervising producer, admits, "Not one of our stronger shows, but it got victimized by circumstances. An enjoyable episode. I think the whole thing with George having back-taxes to pay provided some funny bits that we really liked."

"The problem with that one was more in terms of production than the script. There were some casting problems and way too much story. When you have too much story and a forty-eight-minute show that takes fifty-eight minutes to tell the story, you know you're in trouble," laughs co-story editor Steven Mitchell.

One of executive producer Ken Johnson's goals was to dig deeper into the Tenctonese culture, thus providing greater depth as to who they are as a people. For example, while the feature film told us that the Newcomers were bred as slaves, the pilot and an episode like "The First Cigar" let us know that they were governed by the ruthless Overseers.

"It's a word that comes from our own slave trading in the 1800s," says Johnson. "The people that were in charge of the blacks on the plantations, or on the boats coming over, were called Overseers. On the [space] ship there were Overseers who apparently looked like all the rest of the aliens, except that they had a distinctive tattoo on their wrist, like the S.S. did in World War II, which clearly brands them as—from their point of view—a thing of elevation. From the point of view of the rest of the aliens, it was a mark to be feared. As you would expect, people who have this slave-trading temperament have moved into the sort of underworld society of Los Angeles, and make contact with other people who have their set of values."

Producer Tom Chehak recalls, "Bad casting. That was the first show we actually shot, and in it we cast this heavy-set woman—we wanted a female villain for a change—who was a great actress, but when she got the makeup on, it just didn't work as a Newcomer. It was like this giant pear. That show was really one that could have been stronger. There's an act break where she leaves a bomb behind and blows up all the bad guys.

"What I wanted to do—and this was the kind of influence I would put on all the shows—since she was an Overseer, was to have her drag in another Newcomer who's kind of stoned out. She says, 'Gentlemen, I'm not interested in your deal.' She leaves and they say, 'You better take your stupid, stoned bodyguard with you.' They rip open his shirt and see plastique on his chest, and then the room blows up. That's how I came in and tried to influence the show. Of course, we couldn't do it. It was a fight and the censors were all over our backs. That's the viciousness I wanted to see in an Overseer. It's the villainess of a Nazi S.S. officer. We had to establish that firmly, and not with the normal 'Let's leave a bomb under Hitler's table' thing. Let's do it with blowing up an alien at the same time, with that total disregard for any kind of life."

"Not one of our better shows," opines co-story editor Craig Van Sickle. "That episode kind of ended the first part of the season, the first phase, and things would improve tremendously from that point on."

In contrast, Gary Graham enthuses, "Our very first episode directed by John McPherson, and the noteworthy episode where I met my wife. She played one of the Slag hookers in the early scenes, wearing a blue dress. The first thing she'd ever done playing city atmosphere. I met her when she was made-up as a Slag and sort of asked her out, out of my curiosity—I wanted to see what she looked like without the Slag-head on. Now we've had a baby together."

Eric Pierpoint, with a laugh, adds, "On the fourth day of shooting he sees her, she's in an alien head, and you know the rest. We're all kind of dumbfounded. We kind of said, 'Gee, Gary, you could have taken advantage of the situation for an entire year before settling down.'"

Graham smiles in response, pointing out that there he was, a single guy in Hollywood with a series and the opportunity to just go crazy—and then he goes and meets his wife during production of the first regular episode. "Sort of saved myself from myself," he muses. "As far as the episode itself, Diana Bellamy, for my money, spoke the most effective Tenctonese dialect I've ever heard. She was just great and I think the world of her talent. Other than that, I loved working with John McPherson, who's a great, funny guy. And talented, especially when he got in the squad room. John was coming into his own as a director and he was filled with illusions of grandeur with these long, all-in-one shots. You do four pages of dialogue with one shot. God forbid you have the last line of the shot, because if you blew it you'd go again. The pressure usually fell to me to have the last line in this dreadfully long shot. It looked great in the end and they were great to do."

TVS 07. "THE NIGHT OF SCREAMS"

Original Airdate: October 30, 1989
Writer: Tom Chehak
Director: Gwen Arner
Guest Cast: James Greene (Uncle Moodri)
David Opatoshu (Paul Revere)
Bradford English (Macy)
Meagen Fay (The Coroner)
Mitch Pileggi (Jean-Paul Sartre)
Anya Lilley (Mrs. Sartre)
Steven Majewicz (Tagdot)

Sikes and George are assigned to investigate a series of murders in which the victims were drugged into submission and their hands hacked off above the wrists, resulting in their bleeding to death. The duo find their suspect, an elderly Newcomer playing essentially a Tenctonese version of a Nazi hunter whose target is the Overseers, and his purpose is to seek retribution for the atrocities performed on the slaves. George, while having been sworn to uphold the law, finds himself in the difficult position of agreeing with the man philosophically. Sikes decides to let George call the shots on this one.

NOTE: It unfolds that, on the ship, slaves outnumbered the Overseers ten thousand to one, but they were controlled by the submissive gas and had been manipulated to believe that the Overseers were much more powerful than they really were. In addition, it is learned that George had had a third child, taken by the masters while still on the ship.

As an example of the way the Newcomers have assimilated into human culture, a movie theatre shows an old western dubbed in Tenctonese. Additionally, Sikes uses a Newcomer-English translation device which bears some similarity to *Star Trek*'s Universal Translator, though this one breaks down more often than it works.

Commentary

AUTHOR'S RATING: ***½

"The Night of Screams" provides a terrific intertwining of Tenctonese mythology and our own Halloween traditions. Just the image of Newcomers lying there, dead and handless, is a morbid, unsettling, and macabre sight that fits the mood of the holiday perfectly. The fact that these victims are later revealed to be Overseers only adds poignancy (from the perspective of their killer) to the story that unfolds.

In this installment George goes through an interesting transformation, at first refusing to believe in the myth of Tagdot and then starting to have a change of heart—despite his better judgment—when the body-count begins to rise and the killer's m.o. seems to match that of the Tenctonese demon. There is a nice, tongue-in-cheek moment when George becomes engulfed in this myth and Sikes must remind him, "You're a cop, George, not a comic book."

Also, intriguing background on the Overseers is provided, particularly the fact that they manipulated the slaves into believing that they were all-powerful demons so that their cargo—which outnumbered them many thousands to one—would believe that they were more powerful than they actually were. Real power is added to the scars left behind by the Overseers in the moment when George sees Emily's "costume," an Overseer tattoo on her wrist, and goes berserk. Imagine a Holocaust survivor whose child is wearing a Nazi uniform for Halloween and you'll have some idea of the intensity of the moment.

Eric Pierpoint does a nice job of conveying George's inner turmoil as to how to handle the "Nazi hunter," played here with quiet dignity by veteran performer David Opatoshu. Gary Graham is essentially in support of Pierpoint in this installment, effectively portraying Sikes's concern for George and displaying the heart of the relationship between these two individuals.

Some reality-based humor is found in a climactic moment which occurs in a movie theatre where John Ford's western *My Darling Clementine* (1946) has been dubbed in Tenctonese. Director Gwen Arner deserves special praise, as she establishes a nice sense of atmosphere, particularly in creating the squalor of the life into which many Tenctonese have fallen. Moreover, there is one sequence in a tunnel that is particularly spooky to behold.

Behind-the-Scenes

For executive producer Ken Johnson, "The Night of Screams" was one of the most powerful episodes of *Alien Nation* ever produced, particularly the confrontation between George and the hunter. "There's that moment," he enthuses, "when George says, 'You have the right to remain silent,' and the guy says, 'No one has the right to remain silent! We cannot remain silent. They cannot be judged by Earth laws, because what they did to us must have retribution.' It's a hell of a moment and it puts George absolutely in a vice because, on the one hand, he's sworn to uphold the law, and, on the other hand, George lost a child to the Overseers.

"At the end, I love the scene with George face-to-face with one of the Overseers, having saved him from this 'Nazi hunter,' and George is aiming a gun at this guy. Sikes says, 'I'll be downstairs, George. I don't know what happened here.' So Sikes leaves it to him, and George, honorable man that he is, squeezes the trigger but doesn't fire. We have two or three confrontations like that, where we see this happening and we can, again, deal with the issue of how far you can take the law into your own hands."

"I felt up front that we had to establish the darkness of these Overseers," emphasizes co-producer Tom Chehak. "They're terrible, terrible people. I also tried to push that they live in a real dark part of town. I always tried to explore the Overseers, because they fascinated me. In '[The] Night of Screams,' I put in one that was a drunk, just grabbing people and screwing them on rooftops. Then he meets his end, but still has this attitude to stand up to a Newcomer and say, 'You're dirt, but look what I've been doing on the roof. I'm raping women, I'm drunk, I'm doing whatever I want to do, but you're still dirt.' That's the kind of edge I wanted to bring to those people, but it was all kind of tempered back. That really came from Andy and Diane, who felt we shouldn't go that hard. That was the mix that came to the staff.

"Steve Mitchell, Craig Van Sickle, and myself were all pushing for the darker side of things," he continues. "We all felt that science fiction should be dark, scary, mysterious, and surprising. We always bolted from human stories, feeling that there were much more interesting things going on. I also think the studio was always influencing Kenny, Andy, and

Diane to go away from that kind of [negative] stuff. All of the darkness you saw in *Alien Nation* was really pushed by that side of the staff. The other stuff, the lessons and themes, really came [in particular] from Andy and Diane. I would push the dark side, Andy and Diane would be pushing themes, and Kenny would listen with ears wide open and be a wonderful arbitrator."

Series' supervising producer Andrew Schneider explains, "We wanted to do a Halloween show and a parable about Nazi hunting. Here was a guy, a former slave, who was out killing Overseers, and George was put in a moral bind of having to arrest this guy for something he himself didn't necessarily consider a crime. I think it was a very good show, with some good material about the aliens—particularly Emily—trying to understand Halloween. It had a very moody feel to it, and George's dilemma was very well-portrayed."

"'Screams' combines the best of both worlds," details co-story editor Steven Mitchell. "It's well-produced, well-directed, well-written, well-acted, and it's got an interesting hook to it. We were able to take a very emotional issue for George and combine it with action and the mystery of who the killer is. At the same time, we gave the audience the chance to understand a little bit more about how terrible the conditions were on the slave ship. I think that was really the first step we took to deal with George's emotions and humanity."

Eric Pierpoint admits that the darker-edged *Alien Nation* segments wore him down more during their production. "If it's an eight-day shoot and it's a dark show, you know it's going to be fun, but not as much fun as if you were goofing around and doing a lot more comedy." He adds, "...I think there are some very funny moments when George goes home and Emily has her face in the water, which Susan thinks is bobbing for apples. They're all trying to understand what this

Halloween thing is. Susan has a knife to carve the pumpkin and is just about ready to stab the pumpkin, but feels terrible about it. Emily is very much a kid and wants to do all of the human things that kids do. To her, it's just a big game. So you've got a culture clash going on as well.

"There are times when you invent something on the spot," Pierpoint notes, "and in that one I invented an alien way to speed-read.... We're in the suspect's apartment, and George has a whole bunch of information he has to digest. How's he going to get through this moment? It seems like a little moment that doesn't last more than a couple of seconds on screen, but it's just an indication of how aware you have to be and how sometimes you have to invent on the spot. How is an alien going to read thirty pages of phone numbers and remember them?

"So you invent a way to do it that looks as though it's been part of him forever, and another person's reaction to it might just be a blink. That's the stuff I really like, because that's the stuff that enhances the characters.... I think the audience has more fun kind of catching things in a back-handed sort of way than having it all spelled out for them. But the writers can't think of everything. It's fun as an actor to say, 'Okay, the writers didn't think about this, so how am I going to do it?' Then the writers see it, they put it in their book, and they remember, 'This is how they do this now.'

"But, God, what gruesome stuff in the episode. The shots in the spaceship where you go through this mist and you've got the legend of Tagdot and the cutting-off of hands, and how horrible and treacherous this legend was in our time and how we've turned it into our own folklore. Of course, Nazism is not folklore and can never be folklore because it's too terrible to be folklore. But the 'No one has the right to remain silent' line is great."

Gary Graham smiles slyly when he reflects on this installment. "One of my favorites," he insists. "Directed by Gwen Arner, the first time I'd ever been directed by a woman, before or since. I don't know what it is, I never thought I was an overt chauvinist, but there was something about having a woman director there where I just reverted. She came on the set and from the get-go I was sort of the class clown and she was the substitute teacher, and I gave her a hard time. That's the way I treated her, until I discovered midway through the shoot that not only did she know what she was doing, but she was one of our best directors. She was terrific and I think her work speaks for itself."

TVS 08. "CONTACT"

Original Airdate: November 6, 1989
Writer: Joe Menosky
Director: John McPherson
Guest Cast: Joel Polis (Carl Peterson)
Annabelle Gurwitch (Marissa Meyers)
Jeffrey Josephson (Sergius)
Stuart Fratkin (Bob)
Donald Hotton (Professor Tower)

Professor Tower of the Interplanetary Institute is murdered before he can announce the discovery of a probe/radio source at the outskirts of the galaxy. George and Sikes's suspect is an Overseer who intends to send a signal to that probe, informing "his" people that the slaves have survived and that there are four billion more potential slaves on this planet in the form of humans.

Earlier in the story, Sikes receives a trunk from his late uncle containing a variety of personal mementos that touch his heart and allow him to open up a bit more to Cathy. Meanwhile, George and Susan agree to have another child, this one to be their first Earth-born.

NOTE: This episode was written by Joe Menosky, who served as a story editor on the teleseries *Star Trek: The Next Generation* (1987–94) and, more recently, joined the staff of *Star Trek: Voyager* (1995–).

Commentary

AUTHOR'S RATING: ***½

This is the first episode to really delve into Sikes's background. This is ironic, considering that so much of the segment deals with a never-seen potential threat from deep space. Sikes's knowledge of astronomy is interesting, tying in nicely to his past relationship with his now-late uncle and the arrival of the dead man's telescope. It is that gift which ultimately reawakens him to the wonders of the universe and helps to put him more in touch with his feelings for Cathy.

Both Eric Pierpoint and Terri Treas make clear their longing for a home world they've never seen. Treas, in particular, is a real standout in a closing moment of the show in which she and Sikes are studying the night sky together. Here, she relates how she imagines certain stars are her parents, whom she doesn't remember.

During the course of this episode, a good sense of Earthly racial intolerance is portrayed by an Oriental coroner who refuses to acknowledge George's presence, and a "Humans Only" club, both situations providing Sikes with an opportunity to stand up for his buddy. George, however, is frustratingly tolerant of these racists, until Sikes comments on it. George's explanation of why he puts up with everyone but Sikes is, "I am harder on you not because you are particularly smart, but because I am forced to associate with you on a daily basis. Matt, you are different than they are. You are worth it." This is a very nice moment.

Director John McPherson establishes solid suspense in the episode's final moments as Sikes and George desperately try to stop the Overseer from sending out a signal to the mothership. The partial transmission ends the plot line on an unsettling note, leaving open the question of whether or not there will ever be a response. (As staunch fans of *Alien Nation* are well aware, the question of whether or not there was additional Tenctonese life in the universe was answered several years later in the form of the TV movie *Alien Nation: Dark Horizon.*) Dramatically, the idea posed by this episode was broached first in Ken Johnson's *"V"* series.

Behind-the-Scenes

"When you're doing a show that's science fiction, you don't want to bring in too many actual science-fiction elements," says story editor Craig Van Sickle, with irony. "My fear with 'Contact' was that we were taking a step that opened up our show to not being just about our planet, but other planets as well, and it reminded me of *War of the Worlds* [1953]. That concept is too big and there's too much to explore here before we even begin thinking about what's out there. That was a show that probably would have been better served in the third or fourth season. It turned out to be a fairly effective episode, but we were concerned because we didn't want to do another *'V.'*"

"We wanted to do a story about home and roots," adds *Alien Nation* supervising producer Andrew Schneider. "That's how we got into this whole thing about Sikes, his uncle, and this trunk that had come which he was reluctant to open because of the painful memories attached to it. I think that turned out to be a very good show, and avoided the *'V'* connection."

"Little did we know back then that there would actually be an opportunity to follow up on that," says costar Eric Pierpoint. "The main thing that comes to mind about that episode is when you think about the possibilities of becoming slaves again—the dread of having your whole existence, as you've adapted to it, now come to an end by the possibility of another ship, which George thinks is there. I think it's interesting that in episodes following we didn't carry that in, but the seed was planted. Our fans always wondered 'what if?'.... There's an interesting contradiction between Sikes's fascination with the stars and George's dread of what could happen. Yes, it's fascinating, but wouldn't it be better if we all sat real quiet and didn't make any noise?

"If you go around the slavery and the Nazi thing, you can imagine what would happen. Our own race would sell off our own people, like in Africa. How to use another tribe as a commodity to be bought and sold? You can sense the impending fear and apprehension on George's part about everything being destroyed and you don't understand what, if this was actually something that would come here, the effect would be. I think it's really interesting that he carries such a memory and such a horror of what's out there that he would rather live free on Earth with humans than risk slavery with his own kind.

"I also remember 'Contact' as being the first show where Gary's character was set up as having much of a past in terms of his family," he adds. "So you get a sense of the Sikes character and the bitterness he has about his past."

Gary Graham admits to being fascinated with "Contact," more today than ever, primarily because of the strong (but not yet conclusive) evidence that we on Earth not only have been visited in the past, but might be under present scrutiny by alien intelligence. It is Graham's belief that there is a huge government cover-up: "I saw eyewitness accounts and video accounts and subsequent analysis that makes it pretty compelling that it couldn't really be a hoax," explains Graham. "Plus a close friend of my wife's just told us her eyewitness account that she thought a helicopter was coming over her head. She pulled the car over and this 'helicopter' came over, made no noise other than a slight hum, and she looked up at it and then it split in two and took off. She's a very level-headed CPA. She is *not* a wild-eyed lunatic. She's as honest as the day is long. I love it, because with all of these sightings it makes *Alien Nation* less science fiction and more science speculation.

"For the character," he elaborates, "'Contact' was important because Matt felt abandoned by this uncle when he was thirteen and, in a way, thank God for it, or he wouldn't be the man he is. At the ending, looking into space with Cathy, I have never looked at the stars like that before and, as a metaphor, never looked at Cathy like that before. It was a good way to connect with her, for her to feel my humanity and me to feel her alienness. We established a new bond in that episode. The nuance in the writing, the way they interwove several developing plots that were complete and unto themselves within the episode, but also have a developing through the overall series, was great. The peeling of the onion layers of Sikes's heart was an interesting thing to maintain not only in the episode but throughout the series."

TVS 09. "THREE TO TANGO"

Original Airdate: November 13, 1989
Writers: Diane Frolov and Andrew Schneider
Director: Stan Lathan
Guest Cast: Dana Anderson (May O'Naise)

Alan Scarfe (The Drevni)
Ivan G'Vera (Bjorn)
Charles Hayward (Goran)
Patrick Johnson (Isaac Newton)

Since George and Susan Francisco have agreed to have another child, they ask precinct janitor Albert Einstein to serve as their "Binnaum." It turns out that it takes two Tenctonese males to impregnate a female: the first male, in this case George, provides the seed, while a Binnaum becomes the catalyst which allows conception to occur. Sikes, naturally, has a variety of salacious reactions to the concept, but George chooses to ignore him.

It soon becomes known that Albert was a part of the Binnaum religious sect on the ship, but abandoned it to live as a regular Tenctonese. That order's leader looks upon his serving as catalyst while outside the order as sacrilege, and, as such, he sets about making sure that Albert does not perform this function, even if it means killing him, as this leader has done with others of his kind before.

Sikes and Cathy move a bit closer to a true union, as Sikes questions George about Newcomer erogenous zones and the things that arouse them.

NOTE: Newcomers do not blush. Instead, when embarrassed, their eyes change color.

Commentary

AUTHOR'S RATING: ***

What could have been a routine murder mystery is elevated to a higher level thanks to the insight that is provided into aspects of the Tenctonese culture. The delineation of the sexual practices of the Newcomers is well-handled and fascinating, particularly in contrast to human mores. Interestingly, for all the growth we've seen Sikes undergo to this point, it doesn't take much to nudge him back into being his "old" self as a social bore.

Jeff Marcus shines as the tormented Albert Einstein, who is torn mightily between his desire for a normal life and his cultural obligation as a Binnaum. Refreshingly, here he has the chance to do something besides bumble around the squad room, revealing that there is much more to this Tenctonese than can be assumed at first.

The episode has as its target an unbending religious belief that could, in the worst case, lead to the end of a species *if* the catalysts are wiped out. For the perpetrator of these murders to *not* be a Purist, but rather a Tenctonese religious leader, is an extremely effective plot twist.

The ceremony at episode's end—in which Albert engages with Susan sexually—is tastefully handled. Gary Graham does a brilliant job of giving a sense of awe to Sikes when he sneaks a peek at the couple's coupling. It also opens his eyes to the depths within Cathy, which he demonstrates when he touches her temples affectionately. This lapsed Catholic also makes his way back to the church, having his religious beliefs restored by the sheer faith on George's part.

Behind-the-Scenes

"Another episode we had to do," explains co-story editor Steven Mitchell. "It's November [ratings] sweeps, it's sex, and nothing sells like sex on television. With three-way alien sex, you can't go wrong. And it was one of our most successful episodes in terms of [audience] ratings, which shows you how tawdry America is."

Executive producer Ken Johnson points out that the heart of this episode is really the dichotomy of the Matt-George relationship and their contrasting attitude toward sex. "When George is talking about the fact that it takes a second male to get his wife pregnant, Sikes is immediately dropping into salaciousness. 'Ah, you've got some other guy popping your wife.' And George says, 'You don't understand. You're missing the point of this,' and he finally gets angry and says, 'Look, why don't I tell some Virgin Mary jokes?' So there's a sense of putting Sikes in his place and getting to understand what this is all about. Ultimately it's quite interesting, because the act of mating takes place in a party atmosphere where all your friends and family are invited, which is Newcomer tradition. It's a little surprising to everybody."

Craig Van Sickle, the series' co-story editor, notes, "For the most part it worked. It seems that the Cathy-Sikes relationship kind of started to take a direction at that point. They were side by side during the final ceremony, and there were some really nice looks between the two of them."

"It also dealt with the idea that orthodoxy leads to destruction," interjects the series' supervising producer Andrew Schneider, "via the very idea that the head of these catalysts would be killing his own people and causing their destruction simply because they're not performing their religion correctly. By the way, Kenny was really insistent on having the final ceremony in the episode. The network wanted to shorten that scene, but Kenny was adamant that that was what the show was about and we made it a bigger deal than they originally wanted."

Co-producer Diane Frolov adds, "And then we reflect that kind of intolerance in Sikes's attitude about the Newcomers' sexual practices.... His eventually being able to accept the way the Newcomers procreate enables him to get closer to Cathy and, in fact, his own church. He begins the episode looking at his own church in kind of a small way, and the injustices he felt personally. By the end, he sees the larger picture."

"One of my favorites," enthuses actor Eric Pierpoint. "I think the whole idea is hilarious. When a new culture comes in and introduces these, really, very different takes on what is normal for them versus what is normal for humans, and to have humans exposed to the fact that their morality is opposed to the alien morality that two males impregnate a female, that's just the way it is. But it keys into all kinds of dark, devilish, negative underpinnings of the human culture, where you go from bigamy to 'How can you possibly share your woman like this?'

"One of the most important things about that episode was trying to invent on the spot what this kind of mating ceremony would be. You've got the Binnaum preparing the birth channel and George being the Gannaum hustling Susan upstairs almost as if you're stepping on wine glasses and saying 'mazel tov.' I think there's a feeling of glee and innocence from the aliens' point of view versus this 'Oh, my God, this is disgusting' attitude of the humans. Which I think is great.

"One of the things I like about Gary's character is, in spite of his cynical self, there really is an innocence that is kind of an undercurrent of the things he does. He makes all of these obnoxious statements and conclusions, yet he's really a very open-minded individual underneath it all."

Gary Graham observes, "The sheer lunacy of relating the ceremony in human terms—'Wait a minute, any way you slice it this is a three-way, it's kinky.' It's really an insult to George's whole species to put it in those terms. Once Sikes grounded himself and came back to it in the workaday world of a bumparound, cop-shop mentality, he was pretty insensitive about the whole thing. Sikes goes back to church at the end.

"Apparently I made up my mind at an early age that all religions are rigid and confining and oppressive, which is a prevalent attitude in society today with a lot of people. It may or may not be true. One's relationship with God is a personal thing and people substitute ritual for real, honest contact with the hereafter. In that case I think they're doing themselves and society a disservice. I do appreciate ritual as a means of representing one's very personal and deep-rooted belief in God, but ritual for ritual's sake is at best meaningless and at worst dangerous."

TVS 10. "THE GAME"

Original Airdate: November 20, 1989
Writers: Steven Long Mitchell and
Craig Van Sickle
Director: David Carson
Guest Cast: Sam Anderson (Tom Edison)
Andreas Katsulas (Coolock)
Billy Ray Sharkey (Deon Flack)
Teddy Wilson (Roscoe)
Bill Allen (Ruhtra)
Joel Swetow (Joe Comet)
Isabel Wolfe (Alva Edison)

It is the Day of Descent, celebrating the arrival of the Newcomers on Earth, and George is disturbed by his memories concerning the Game. This was a Russian-Roulette-like Overseer sport on the mothership, involving jet-powered sprays of salt water that burned holes through the chests of its victims. Now, several recent homicides indicate that the Game has been put back into practice on Earth. George is determined to stop it at all costs, simultaneously resolving his own nightmares while confronting the Overseer Coolock, "host" of the Game on the ship as well as on Earth.

Commentary

AUTHOR'S RATING: ****; *Alien Nation* at its best!

"The Game" is one of the most organic episodes of the entire series. It effectively brings the viewer deep inside the Tenctonese culture while "disguising" the tale in an action-adventure format. Having a Day of Descent holiday commemorating the Newcomers' arrival on Earth is the perfect contrivance, and the accompanying celebration very much feels like a real holiday.

Andreas Katsulas brings a wonderful sense of arrogance and power to his role as Coolock—an Overseer who obviously enjoyed his position on the slave ship and refuses to relinquish any of it just because he's stranded on Earth.

Eric Pierpoint gives an especially solid performance here as George Francisco. At first, he is depressed about the Day of Descent, then tortured by memories of the Game on the ship, and, ultimately, horrified by the discovery that it's now being played on Earth. His final confrontation with Coolock is electric in its power as he forces the Overseer to play *the* Game. For a moment, the viewer is left wondering whether or not George will actually kill this individual.

Of special interest is a moving scene in the precinct locker room, where George breaks down and tells Sikes about his experience on the ship with the Game. He explains how he lost his brother to it and his resultant guilt for surviving, as he was in the midst of playing when the ship entered Earth's atmosphere—thus is provided an explanation for his ongoing depression. Gary Graham is at his most sensitive, initially hugging George as he cries, and ultimately holding his hand while his partner details what transpired on the ship.

David Carson, a frequent director of *Star Trek* who would ultimately direct the feature film *Star Trek: Generations* (1994), proves himself here to be the show's best director, successfully creating moments of suspense during the playing of the Game. Even with little budget with which to work, he sparks the viewers' imagination as to what life on the Tenctonese slave ship must have been like. This is true artistic creativity.

As to the character of George Francisco, it was earlier revealed that he had a third child taken from him by the Overseers and, now, that he has lost his brother to the Game. One must ask, how has he managed to maintain his sanity?

Behind-the-Scenes

"Quite frankly," comments co-story editor Steven Mitchell, "this was one of the few times in television where everything came together. We are extremely proud of this script, and it's probably among the best work Craig and I have ever done. We were very lucky to get David Carson as director, because he brought it to life in ways that we hadn't imagined, giving it a look and vision. It's a very intense show to watch. When you've written it, know exactly what's going to happen, and you're *still* nervous when you're watching, you know it works.

"Another level that made it better is that most shows in hour-TV peak by the end of the third act, and then slide down in the fourth. In this case, by the time we hit the fourth act we were still climbing that mountain of emotion and there was still a major surprise to be revealed. The final conflict—and I don't think we had a better ending on any show—got you thinking, taking you to a level of understanding what kind of people the Newcomers were to survive this kind of mistreatment. Basically, you realize it ain't *Alf*, and that you're putting your character through a real emotional ringer and a lot of development.

"There was a lot of resistance to doing that show," he

adds. "There was a big battle going on inside because the other producers, except for Tom, were very nervous about doing something that intense. Afterward, we only got away with a couple of shows that were near that level. We pushed for it, because that's what the show should be like."

Co-story editor Craig Van Sickle explains, "For my money, 'The Game' evokes a reaction in the audience. Like it or not, it gives you the action on a gut, emotional level. When you accomplish something like that, it's like getting ringers in horseshoes. Even as uncomfortable as Ken Johnson was with that show, he told us the story about a woman who came up to him a week after it aired—at the NATPE convention—and said, 'I really loved "The Game." It made me throw up.' She was serious. It was *that* intense. Not that I want all of our episodes to make people throw up, but there's so much pablum on TV that when you can really make somebody react emotionally and become involved, I think you've gone above and beyond. I think that's what we all shoot for, and in twenty-two episodes you're only going to do that a third of the time."

"It had all the darkness that I wanted to see the show have," producer Tom Chehak notes. "The flashbacks, I think, were really well done. The network didn't want us to do flashbacks anymore after that episode, because they didn't want us to do science fiction. They wanted us to lose the science-fiction edge. They felt the science fiction audience is a limited one, and said, 'Don't do flashbacks, because it takes us out of real time.' These are the things you fight constantly. Great episode. The guys wanted [this to be] a gladiator show and I backed them all the way, saying, 'Yeah, let's do [*The*] *Deer Hunter* [1978].'"

Andrew Schneider, supervising producer, enthuses, "Very powerful, well-directed, and well-written. Certain people get depressed around the holidays. George has this terrible memory of what happened to him, just before he is about to celebrate this great moment that the Newcomers hold dear. It's really about exorcising the past and learning how to continue with life. A lot of people agree that it's one of our best episodes."

Gary Graham is one of them. "Great show and it was pretty cool to film the Game machine that our poor special-effects guys couldn't get to function quite right," he laughs. "It drove the director, David Carson, crazy. He's a mild-mannered Englishman, but boy did we bring out the ire in him that day, about the fourteenth time when the cameras were rolling and the thing wouldn't quite function properly. We finally got it working, but it took a long time to get there, with a lot of screaming and shouting. Very frustrating.... The episode represented heavy stuff for Eric to dredge up, going through his past and the horror of the Game when it was played on the ship. I saw that episode as being more in support of my partner."

"Gary's right about the problems with that gizmo," interjects Eric Pierpoint. "The thing was supposed to spin a lot better than it did. We had a guy underneath the table trying to spin the thing around. It was supposed to be like a Swiss watch, but ended up being more like a Forty-seventh-Street-and-Fifth-Avenue fake Rolex for $9.95."

The actor was pleased with the richness of the details provided about George's background. "I always thought George was a combination of being amazingly capable and potentially violent, having a dark side that can really take care of business when it's necessary. There's something very powerful in the containment of that intensity. It's not displayed very often, but when it is, it's kind of laser-guided so that he is sitting on a powder keg, having had all of these terrible things happen to him, and having sat across the table and watched people die. And having his younger brother killed and wanting to go in his place. We had a great time chewing up the scenery. I love the rawness of that show."

TVS 11. "CHAINS OF LOVE"

Original Airdate: November 27, 1989
Writers: Diane Frolov and Andrew Schneider
Director: Harry Longstreet
Guest Cast: Bennett Liss (Ralph Emerson)
Darren Dalton (Leonard)
Teddy Wilson (Dr. Roscoe Brennan)
Theodore Raimi (Johnny Appleseed)
Caitlin O'Heaney (Jenny Hoffat/Clara Bow)
Jeffrey Nordling (Ted Healy)
Thom Zimerele (Daniel)
John Hese (Lance Lot)
S. A. Griffin (Marvin Gardens)
Diana Barton (Emma Bovary)

In this variation of the motion picture *Sea of Love* (though the episode aired before the feature film was released in 1989), Newcomer Clara Bow is thought to be a "Black Widow" killer, mating with and then murdering sexual partners she meets through a computer dating service. These crimes are revealed to be the work of Ted Healy, a former obsessed lover of hers who can't stand the thought of her being with anyone else. As such, he's lined up his next target: George Francisco, currently involved in a sting operation.

The on-again, off-again Sikes-Cathy relationship veers off a bit in this segment when he tries to get her to watch some Three Stooges comedy films, and she, like ninety-nine percent of all human females, doesn't think they're amusing at all. Complicating his life even further is Tenctonese Marvin Gardens, who has taken a bonding drug and fallen in love with him—the same bonding drug that an insecure George wants Susan to ingest.

NOTE: On the ship, the Overseers chose mates for their

slaves, George and Susan happening to fall in love despite this fact. This episode's killer, Ted Healy, is an inside-joke for Three Stooges fans. Healy was the name of the performer who discovered the trio.

Commentary

AUTHOR'S RATING: **½
What might have proved to be merely a routine murder mystery gains importance by the introduction of Sardonac, the Tenctonese bonding drug.

Sikes getting as upset as he does over Cathy not enjoying the Three Stooges is blown *way* out of proportion. If human females think that the Stooges are morons, why should the Tenctonese be any different? There's also a conceptual problem about George getting *so* obsessed over Clara Bow's photo that he begins acting like those who have taken the drug, which makes the situation seem not too plausible. There is, however, some humor (and intended irony, given her Earth name of Clara Bow) gained when George meets the woman in the photo and discovers that she is a *bumbo* (a.k.a. bimbo).

What works best in this episode is George's insecurity over his relationship with Susan, as he fears he may lose her and wants them to bond. Thankfully, he realizes that they actually fell in love naturally (more or less) and that this is the most important element in their relationship. There are also great comic moments mined from Marvin Gardens taking Sardonac and "bonding" with Sikes. (An additional sense of irony is found in the taking of the name "Marvin Gardens" from the early game of Monopoly.) Gary Graham is hysterical playing Sikes's exasperation over the situation, and brings home the point that Sikes is the *last* person in the world who would want a male—Tenctonese or human—to come on to him.

Behind-the-Scenes

"One of my favorites," smiles supervising producer Andrew Schneider. "The theme... is that love is only love when it's free. Love enslaved is not really love, which is reinforced on several levels, one with Sikes and Cathy. If she won't like the Three Stooges, he finds it hard to accept her on this one level, and by having this Newcomer attach to him because of this drug, he realizes that you have to *give* people love if you're going to love them, and vice versa. George has the whole thing where he becomes fascinated with the portrait of this beautiful woman, which makes him fear his commitment to Susan. His resolution to make Susan take the drug wouldn't be true love. Real love is a risky business, and there are no guarantees."

"An okay episode," counters co-story editor Steven Mitchell, "but not one of my personal favorites. I think 'Screams' and 'The Game' are pretty much on a different level and deeper. You look at television, on a series you'll have eight or ten that are really good and the rest are okay. 'Chains of Love' was a good show, but if you could only pick one *Alien Nation* to see again, I don't think it would be this one."

"I *know* it wouldn't be," observes the other story editor, Craig Van Sickle. "For the most part it carried you along, but it was a middle-lane episode that you're going to have in the course of a season."

Co-producer Tom Chehak points out, "Funnily enough, there was that movie with Al Pacino after we produced this one, *Sea of Love,* which people say was exactly like this episode. I think that 'Chains of Love' got diluted somewhere along the line. It never really was a standout for me."

Sikes is *extremely* uncomfortable through much of this installment, which isn't particularly surprising, as one would imagine the character to be something of a homophobe who would be put off by Marvin's advances.

Per Gary Graham, "As I explain to people, it's possible to be repulsed by something without being frightened of it. In all seriousness, it was so much fun to do. I laughed openly when I read the script. The whole notion of me being the first one he sees is just hilarious. Matt not being the most sensitive and understanding guy in the world, of course. I loved the way it was written and the way we pulled it off [by] eventually kind of feeling sorry for the guy. He can't help it. Matt says, 'Look, you're not a bad-looking guy, you'll find someone.' And then it's kind of, 'What am I saying?' Very funny stuff."

Eric Pierpoint found it interesting that in "Chains of Love" George is experiencing jealousy for the first time. "He doesn't like it and wants to eliminate it," says the actor. "Also, being attracted to another female, until he finds out she's a *bumbo*, Clara Bow, and George becoming fascinated by an image. I remember we were tossing around ideas, 'What is stimulating? What are the erogenous zones on aliens?' On a previous show, I was describing it to Matt and talked about the bridge of the nose, the armpits, spots, whatever. I remember sitting there in the station, looking at a picture of Clara Bow, and kind of distractedly and absent-mindedly stroking the bridge of my nose while looking at the picture. I don't know if the fans caught that, but it was deliberate. I looked at that and thought, 'What if George is caught in a semi-masturbatory situation?' Very subtle, but he catches himself, looks around, stops doing it, and puts the picture down very embarrassed. It was one of those things that was out there that I was really curious whether or not people would pick up on it.... Overall, it was a light show and kind of fluffy."

TVS 12. "THE RED ROOM"

Original Airdate: December 18, 1989
Writers: Steven Long Mitchell and Craig Van Sickle
Director: Chuck Bowman
Guest Cast: John P. Connelly (Jeffries)
Ray Reinhardt (Dr. Chris Pettit)
Katherine Justice (Dr. Marcie Wright)
Michelle Lamar Richards (Dr. Lois Allen)
Tom Dugan (Silas Marner)
Chuck Bennett (Marcus Byer)

George and Sikes investigate a series of murders, but are removed from the case when the FBI becomes involved and claims jurisdiction. "Project Dart" is discussed briefly, and the words have a powerful impact on George, who is haunted by dim recollections of something horrible. Through hypnosis, he reveals that while in quarantine after the Newcomers landed on Earth, he and a group of fellow Tenctonese were brainwashed by the United States government to be made into perfect killing machines. The "programming" didn't work on George, who had an ethical imprint they could not penetrate, but one of those machines has decided now to fight back against the people pulling the strings, exterminating them one by one.

While all this is going on, Sikes tries to avoid a mandatory psychological examination because he doesn't want to allow anyone to get that close to him (which is actually part of his problem in relating to Cathy). George, on the other hand, looks forward to the exam, though he's disappointed by the resulting conclusion: he's a "control freak."

NOTE: There's a nice moment when Sikes looks at a dead body and mutters, "Andarko," rather than "God." This simple moment demonstrates how constant involvement with Newcomers is affecting him in subtle ways, all of which is being observed by George.

Commentary

AUTHOR'S RATING: ***½; *Alien Nation* meets *The Manchurian Candidate*

Character and more character is evident as Sikes and George gain some insights into themselves.

Gary Graham effectively displays Sikes's inability to honestly express his feelings, his reluctance to do so saying much more about his background than any dialogue could. The final moments of the segment delve into Sikes's mind and are extremely effective: There is a party going on in another room—whose participants include Cathy—and Sikes demonstrates his inability simply to open the door and join the others.

In turn, Eric Pierpoint runs a true gamut of emotions in this episode. At first he is upset at being classified as "anal" and "obsessive," and then must deal with the unfolding mystery of his involvement in "Project Dart" and the "Red Room."

The greatest irony of this installment, of course, is that George (now adding having been brainwashed to the loss of his brother and child) is mentally healthier than Sikes might ever be. The script and Chuck Bowman's direction keep things moving at a steady clip, achieving several extremely suspenseful sequences in the midst of all the character-development material.

Behind-the-Scenes

Story editor Steven Mitchell emphasizes, "That final shot, which was choreographed in the editing by Tom Chehak, has a real nice answer to why Sikes is afraid of looking at himself and why he's afraid of taking the next step with Cathy. We thought that was a real nice touch."

"We're very proud of this one," explains Mitchell's fellow story editor Craig Van Sickle, "and it works on a few different levels, both as intense entertainment in the Red Room and what it means, and again on a personal level with both of our guys—Sikes, who's avoiding the psychiatrist and afraid to talk about himself, and George, who has some dark secret inside that he can't seem to express. I know this was one of Eric Pierpoint's favorite episodes. He really thought it had explored his character more than most of them."

"After that episode," adds Mitchell, "Eric came up to our office, closed the door, and basically thanked us for that script. He was so happy with it and enjoyed it. We also got good feedback from professionals in the psychiatric areas who have written to us to say how they appreciate the approach we took to their profession. The show basically represented the tone we pretty much went for in every script we did. 'The Game' and 'The Red Room' were basically the way we thought the show should be done. One of the wonderful things about working with Ken Johnson is that he let all of us have our own distinct point of view. There was give-and-take on everything, but if you really felt passionate about something, he would let you run with it. We'll always be eternally grateful to him for giving us that."

"Good episode," judges producer Tom Chehak, "dealing with mind control and the dark side of what is trapped in George's brain. The network was always giving us this hard time about being careful about science-fiction material. I should say that this command came down later on. It didn't happen right away. By the end of the season they were saying, 'Get rid of the science-fiction elements, and give us more of the family side of things.' That's what they wanted to do, and they're the ones paying the bills."

Producer Andrew Schneider says, "'The Red Room' was sort of our [*The*] *Manchurian Candidate* [1962]. I think our feeling afterward was that we had put George through the ringer over the season. The poor guy's had one lousy experience after another."

Which is exactly what Eric Pierpoint enjoyed most about the series entry. "I like it because it had a lot to do with George's other side," he relates. "There was something so haunting and so well done for series television. Again, you get those funny moments of things that happen from the character. At the beginning of the episode we had the new psychologist who was coming in and evaluating everybody. Matt can't write down six things that make sense, while George has pretty much typed out a dissertation on himself and...handed it in to the psychologist, who rejects it because she says he has gone way overboard with it. He answers the questions as though he were trying to take the Nobel Prize for peace or something, and is accused of being very anal. Which he is, but, as he puts it, if she knew anything about Newcomer biology, she would know that would be an impossibility.

"It becomes an interesting look at the contrasts between George and Sikes," he continues. "George becomes an open book eventually and is, in a lot of ways, a lot more accessible, and Matt is going to be eternally alone and is so damaged on an emotional level that if he can ever reveal anything and get his life together, it will be a miracle. He is typical of human men. The evolution of the characters was something we were very conscious of during the course of the series. With

George, I wanted to take what I thought were the best elements of being human and inject those elements into the character and work from there. So he becomes almost too good to be true in many ways. He can be a combination of Robert Young, James Bond, and Tony Randall. It's a very strange combination, but those are the things I imaged in my mind. I thought everybody loves a fool, everybody loves a hero. I remembered how frustrated 1950s fathers appeared to be. He's kind of ineptly going about his home life like that too, but then the complications come out when you really see the layers that have constructed the character because of 'The Red Room' and 'The Game' (TVS 10) and what he's been through. You can put him in almost any situation and understand how he came to be.

"With Matt, I think he had a drunken father that used to beat him, an uncle that left him, an unsuccessful marriage, a daughter who only came around one time. All of that made him alone and kept him alone, and as a result he and George are opposites. After time goes by, I think it's natural to risk going in the other direction. He eventually becomes a little more stable with Cathy, and...as *Alien Nation* has gone on [in the form of TV movies], Matt and George are reacting to each other as beings, not necessarily because of cultural differences. It's truly *The Odd Couple.* Their personalities is what's attractive and repulsive at times, rather than necessarily always being a culture clash; it's the chemistry. It's all the good stuff that's ever been written about opposites teaming up like that. That's what's fun."

Gary Graham views "The Red Room," just as was the case with "The Game," as an episode in which he plays in true support of his partner, though he did enjoy his character's bouts with the psychologist. In fact, mention of this segment brings to the surface his deeply-held feelings about the fields of psychiatry and psychotherapy.

"Shrinks in general just want to get in and monkey around and create stuff that ain't even there, and by the time you get through with them you've got stuff in there that wasn't there before you began," he opines. "It's my belief that to a large degree some of the psychiatric community is interested in turning over stones and, in their never-ending quest to discover neuroses and psychoses, inadvertently create some of their own. People will 'remember' things that never happened with certain auto-suggestions they think maybe did happen. Under the right drugs and right hypnotic circumstances, man, I can recount past lives and past abuses and come up with a further reason to not take responsibility for my own life. I think it feeds to a general malaise in this country of victimness, of avoidance of responsibility—the whining of America. It was always somebody else's fault, somebody did it to me back then and that's why I'm here and why society's screwed up. I throw a flag on that play and say, 'C'mon people, it's just another excuse to step down and abdicate your responsibility and your rights.'"

TVS 13. "THE SPIRIT OF '95"

Original Airdate: January 15, 1990
Writer: Tom Chehak
Director: Harry Longstreet
Guest Cast: Mark Thomas Miller (Wyatt Earp)
Henry Brown (Jesse Parker)
Mark Joy (Max Klay)

Susan and Buck decide to become heavily involved in politics, as an amendment to the constitution which guarantees equal rights for Newcomers is soon to be voted on throughout the land.

A series of attacks is launched on campaign headquarters and important Newcomers are involved in the ongoing struggle, resulting in a growing sympathy for the Tenctonese. Everyone blames the Purists, but Sikes and George aren't so easily convinced. In the meantime, Sikes, who has been drafted as the leader of his building's tenant association, learns of the necessity of the democratic system, even on such a basic level.

NOTE: This is the last episode in which Dobbs, Burns, and Jill would be billed as series regulars. Undoubtedly, these little-used characters were only included in the first thirteen episodes due to their initial contracts.

Commentary

AUTHOR'S RATING: **½

A real highlight of this episode is an intense sequence in the precinct interrogation room between Sikes, George, and Purist leader Max Klay, where they debate Tenctonese rights. The latter person displays the hypocrisy of using the Bible as a rationale for the Newcomers not belonging on this planet. The Purists' belief is that humanity was placed here on Earth by God and is destined to rule this world—though one could wonder whether or not the arrival of the Tenctonese could be a part of divine intervention as well.

Tension increases later when George enters Purist headquarters. It's a short scene, but one of the strongest ever presented on the *Alien Nation* series. Pierpoint balances revulsion with his sense of purpose as he steps into the lion's den amidst softly-whispered murmurs of "Slag."

It's also refreshing to see Sikes maturing so nicely, the experience of this episode allowing him to take responsibility for himself as a citizen and as a member of the community, particularly in terms of the tenant association.

The revelation that all of the attacks on the Newcomers' political headquarters are Tenctonese-based rather than Purist is a real turnabout, though our "faith" in the human supremacists is ultimately restored in a final twist.

To be specially noted is the cute "Stooge continuity" as Matt walks down the hallway to Cathy's apartment, with the sounds of Three Stooges mayhem coming from his apartment.

Behind-the-Scenes

"I was going to direct that one and wanted to write a rather simple episode," details producer Tom Chehak. "I wanted to bring forth Susan and Buck's involvement and a family-oriented show. I really designed the episode around the family as well as the cop shop. I wanted to get our people politically active again, like they were in the pilot. A straightforward show, but not a standout."

Story editor Craig Van Sickle says, "That was a show that just never found its voice. The trouble is that Tom wrote that and was supposed to direct. I think a lot of ideas he had in his head, which would have been brought to life, he never had a chance to do because ultimately it was assigned to somebody else. So, unfortunately, a lot of it kind of got left out. That's not knocking him at all. It's more of a compliment. It just never came together. Also, looking back, it seems that we were under some big time constraints with the schedule, and just getting it done was a positive thing in itself."

"[We were] just trying to look at government, democracy, and the process of government through an alien's eyes," notes producer Diane Frolov. "Sikes really takes it for granted and George, being a former slave, can't understand his attitude. The Newcomers treasure this freedom that they have. It's also about the idea that with freedom comes responsibility."

When told of Frolov's comments about the episode, actor Gary Graham smiles, responding, "That's why I walk and talk and hit marks, and they write. They are brilliant and articulate, and I live to serve. She is absolutely right. I've done a lot of world travel and I would talk to friends who have never been out of California about my newfound appreciation for the American system of government, liberty, and individual liberties. And the notion that freedom is only as good as the amount of responsibility you're willing to exercise to maintain it. They just sort of look at me like, 'Will you get off it?' Most of my friends would come up with denigrating things to say about our leadership and our system. My unspoken attitude was always, 'If you don't like it here, go try it in some other country, see what their problems are, and then we'll talk.' It's not until you really get out and move around in the world and see what systems there are out there that you come back and just kiss the ground when you land at LAX.

"So Sikes has lived in this system, he's taken it for granted, he doesn't vote, he's bitter. And here's a guy who comes from another solar system and he's the one who says, 'Don't you realize that this is great how you've set it up? You've got these great checks and balances, and these inalienable—which takes on new meaning with George—rights, and it's a privilege to vote.' It's a fun, fun show, plus our system isn't a straight democracy, it's mob rule. It's a representative republic. Anyone who studies the government exhaustively knows that it was set up ingeniously. I'm chagrined because I see constant dissemblance of a very brilliant system that had checks and balances, and always held the greatest reverence toward individual liberties and freedoms.

"The founding fathers realized that freedom should be sacrosanct if our political experiment here called the United States is to have any value at all. I think Sikes in this episode comes to appreciate the political situation. He has to handle all these disparate points of view and ultimately accepts it. Hey, every week for me was 'What's Sikes's problem this week and how does he come out just a little more evolved?' One more step from Neanderthal."

Considering "The Spirit of '95" to be a middle-of-the-road episode of *Alien Nation*, Eric Pierpoint, nonetheless, enjoyed the moment in the episode where George has to enter Purist headquarters as part of his investigation. "I always loved taking George into volatile situations like that one," he says. "You really get a sense of isolation when you walk into the lion's den. You just try to use your imagination and think about what it would be like for a black man to walk into a place of power in the South fifty years ago. Or a white face in Harlem. Or go down to L.A., South Central, and walk in their territory.

"I do remember that happened to me in Washington, D.C., having that feeling. When I was sixteen or seventeen, I was picking up something in an area that I didn't feel comfortable in because I was the only white person in the area and was feeling that it was not my territory. I was apprehensive. There were a couple of guys who came up to the car as I started driving, and I thought, 'What do they want?' and I felt the hairs stick up on the back of my head. They stopped the car, looked out the window, and they said, 'Just wanted to tell you that your side door is open.'

"I remember I had a real rush from that. It was only because I wasn't used to being in that kind of situation. That's what it was like and what it would have been like for aliens to land on Earth and be looked at with a mixture of hostility and curiosity. You just don't know. If you know you're going into a hostile environment and shouldn't be there, it can only mean using your imagination and figuring it out. So I liked that part of the episode."

TVS 14. "GENERATION TO GENERATION"

Original Airdate: January 29, 1990
Writers: Andrew Schneider and Diane Frolov
Director: John McPherson
Guest Cast: James Greene (Uncle Moodri)
Timothy Scott (Lowell Bratigan)
Scott Jaeck (Henry Glass)
Francis Guinan (Howard Thayer)
Ryan Cutrona (Dunaway)

A series of murders in which the victims are burned to death is tied to a mysterious Tenctonese box that keeps transferring from person to person. George is shocked to learn that one of the people involved in the killing is Uncle Moodri, who is a member of the Elders, the Newcomers chosen to keep the old ways alive in the minds of future generations.

The search for the box intensifies, with Sikes and George finally coming to understand its importance to the memory of the Tenctons' home planet.

As a subplot, Sikes becomes a big brother to a youth, first to avoid weekend police duty, and then because he realizes the importance of reaching out to others in need.

NOTE: This episode reveals that Sikes was born and raised in Detroit, and has a deathly fear of spiders.

Commentary

AUTHOR'S RATING: ***

Like the majority of *Alien Nation* episodes, "Generation to Generation" features a crime story—in this case, the theft of the Tenctonese box—but is more concerned with how the thematic elements of that part of the story impact on the characters.

Once again, James Greene's truly eccentric Uncle Moodri is the one person who makes perfect sense in his concerns that the current generation maintain its connection to the past and, ultimately, pass it on to the next.

Gary Graham continues to excel at humanizing Sikes, recognizing that he's been a failure as a "big brother" and ultimately coming to realize the power of the gift he's been given—a child whose life he can influence. At the same time, Eric Pierpoint's George is extremely dismissive of Moodri's rantings about the box, until the man dies for his beliefs. At episode's end, when the Elders use the box to transport George and Sikes to a virtual version of Tencton, it is an extremely touching moment, thanks to the actors' sense of awe. Pierpoint is particularly effective in conveying the feeling that George has, at last, come "home."

Behind-the-Scenes

"The theme," points out producer Andrew Schneider, "is that you must sacrifice for the generations to come, and it happened on several levels. George's Uncle Moodri gave his life for that box, which was so important to his people on many levels, and Sikes's lesson was becoming a big brother. First he took on the job to get out of some duty, and by the end he realized it was a great thing."

"The emotional impact at the end with the box really worked for me," says story editor Steven Mitchell. "We learned a little more about the planet [Tencton]. I also loved the idea that looking into this box takes you back home or to a place you've never been. It's like being from Africa or something, and your only chance to see your homeland is through this box."

"The only thing I would have done differently in that

episode, would have been more of what happens when the box falls into the wrong hands," says co-story editor Craig Van Sickle. "We saw that someone had the shit burned out of them, but I would have liked to have seen more of that and the darker elements of it. I think some of us fell into a trap where we had a good idea, but the execution wasn't at a level of intensity that it could have been. It would still be an okay show, better than average, but there were areas where it could have been better. I guess everybody is guilty of that."

It should be noted that some staff members had already indicated their own self-imposed censorship of science-fiction ideas, knowing that the network would veto those creative flights of fancy anyway.

"In some respects, that happened," says Mitchell, "but in other respects, I still think that some of the self-censorship would have happened regardless. For instance, in 'Fountain of Youth' we probably could have gone a little deeper into it, but early on you take these things slower. What Craig and I tried to do with our scripts was make them work on different levels, with each level giving us a different emotion to explore. We were fortunate, if that's what you want to call it, in that we never had any stories rejected by the network. I would certainly call our shows right up there as intense science fiction.

"On the one hand," he elaborates, "there was some self-censoring going on. On the other, I think a lot of it had to do with the evolution of the story, the pitching of it to the network, and the knowledge that the actual execution of it had to be there as well. If the network was in the mood for a cop show, we would basically pitch the cop elements, knowing what we wanted to do emotionally. Then when they were in the mood for emotion, we would pitch the emotional elements, keeping our cop elements down. For us to pitch an episode over the phone could take five minutes, but they wouldn't have any idea what the nuances were or how it would be played out, although we did. We know that if you want a show with a lot of comedy, we're going to pitch you a lot of comedy, even if there are darker moments in the show.

"When the final product is delivered to the studio, they say, 'These guys delivered. It has the comedy elements we wanted, but it also has a, b, c, and d.' That's just good, creative business to do it that way. You could dissect a show in the story stage and never get anywhere, especially with who we finally called 'The Suits' at the studio. They have to trust that you can deliver, and in our case we did, so we didn't have any problems. We gave them what they wanted and a whole lot more. It's kind of like a basketball game. You're about to shoot and the coach says, 'Don't shoot, don't shoot.' You do it anyway. It goes in and he says, 'Good shot.' As long as you deliver, that's all that really matters."

"I loved that episode," Gary Graham enthuses, "because I enjoyed working with the kid. He was a real sweetie. In my own personal life I wasn't a father by then but was yearning to be one. My sister had a couple of little kids. I was Uncle Gary and it sort of hit my alarm clock and said, 'It's about the time in your life when you really need to be a dad.' It just kind of occurred to me. Maybe that triggered my yearning for a significant other and starting a family. We started a family not long after that, maybe a year or so later. Art imitating life? It's the other way around. I watch television to figure out how I'm going to live."

Eric Pierpoint adds, "The preservation of culture and the selling-out of culture was the issue. It means a lot of things. The price of greed is the death of a culture. On the other hand, if you embrace the culture you can reap tremendous rewards and it can have a stabilizing effect on your own cultural soul. Moodri was the example, the Joan of Arc or the sacrificial lamb, not that he had a contract-negotiation problem, which would have been an easy way out. The sacrifice with his death was important.

"Going to Tencton was a big thing," he adds. "I remember people were describing what Tencton should be like and said we would be using blue screen, which wasn't used very often in episodic television. It was a real question and a real interesting experience shooting that. You're on the blue-screen stage trying to figure out what you're looking at, and you don't know because it isn't there. You haven't seen the rendition and you're looking at nothing. That's the part of acting that I think is such a challenge. Here we are, now you're looking at the moons of Tencton, how do you feel about that? What kind of joy and awe are you feeling? It's double acting.

"Acting normally, at least you're emoting across from something. When you're across from something that's really not there, it's going one step further and it's a complete make-believe situation. For the character, George's going to Tencton was both uplifting and devastating. At the same time, with the peace he's found on Earth, he's moving forward and taking his family with him."

TVS 15. "EYEWITNESS NEWS"

Original Airdate: February 5, 1990
Writers: Charles S. Kaufman, Larry B. Williams, Steven Long Mitchell, and Craig Van Sickle
Director: Lyndon Chubbock
Guest Cast: Angela Bassett (Renee Longstreet)
Rob King (Louis Denton)
Deborah Goodrich (Virginia Hamm)

Gene Butler (Arvin Kaufman)
Hugh McGuire (Ernie Denton)
Ian Patrick Williams (John)
Jennifer Roach (Tilly)
David Hoskins (Joe)

Exploitation is the name of the game as George Francisco becomes the focus of a local news station's special report on the life of a Newcomer police officer, with a follow-up on his activities for an entire week. George becomes egocentric with all the attention, alienating his family and Sikes, while his work begins to suffer. Concurrently, Sikes and George are assigned the case of Newcomer Virginia Hamm, performer in a video phone-sex-line service, who has been violently assaulted by a pair of teenagers using the service because their father has done the same.

Sikes and Cathy discuss the sexuality of both humans and Tenctonese, each expressing curiosity about the other. While not taken any further in this episode, there is the sense that they are moving closer to having a serious relationship.

NOTE: Certain sounds, including that of the FCC's Emergency Broadcasting System, are extremely sexually-stimulating to the Tenctonese.

Commentary

AUTHOR'S RATING: **

While it's amusing to watch George's transition from reluctance to being featured in the news story to it becoming the very essence of his existence, there is really little else to recommend in this episode. *Alien Nation*'s usual approach is to tackle a subject matter and illuminate it for the viewer. While "Eyewitness News" tackles pornography and phone sex, its ultimate message that parents shouldn't view pornography or their kids might too, is pretty simplistic stuff. For other shows this could be deep "message" material, but for this series it's kind of simplistic and meaningless.

Behind-the-Scenes

"A complete rewrite of an outside writer," notes story editor Craig Van Sickle. "You know how all the elements of 'The Game' came together so wonderfully? This was one situation, for whatever reason, that the return was a nightmare. First of all, the biggest problem was with Standards and Practices. They were just terrified of this video phone-sex line. The ultimate message went beyond titillation, and we were trying to convince Standards and Practices that we could do that. It was essentially '976' over a television."

"Many people who come into this country are exploited," interjects co-story editor Steven Mitchell. "We got about seventy-five percent of what we could have gotten. The ironic thing is that if we had somebody with a machine gun who killed everybody, that would have been fine. But if there's a kid watching sex who's affected by it, we couldn't do that. We didn't understand what the argument was."

Producer Tom Chehak offers, "We attempted to explore freedom of speech, and I think there was a lot of fence-sitting. In the original script, we tried to take a side, which I fought for. I thought that if pornography is out there, people have a right to see it. You have to make a stand for that just as strongly as you make a stand against it. Not that I'm for pornography, but I think people should be allowed to watch it if that's what they want. I think what that script missed a lot in the early drafts is that we weren't presenting the other side clearly or fairly enough. As writers, of course we all have the feeling that we don't want our children watching pornography. It was a pretty difficult episode, and I think we consider it our clunker."

"Exploitation, plain and simple," says producer Andrew Schneider. "How the media exploits us and how we exploit ourselves. The episode said that when you dehumanize people, it will lead to violence. It was a very hard show to produce, and I think in some ways it suffered a little from that. We could have used another day or two of production."

"The funny thing about the episode," laughs Eric Pierpoint, "is the transformation in George. He doesn't want to be a celebrity to begin with, but then he starts to like it. He starts to enjoy it so much that it's like, 'Matt, can you please stand out of my light?' I think it's funny how Matt gets incredibly frustrated because George is getting a bigger head than he has and is constantly leaving him flat. George is such an innocent in many ways.

"Like anybody else, he's presented with an idea that's troubling at first, but then it looks like he can make a lot of money from it. I remember the most fun part of that show was watching George running that string out much too far and trying to reel him in. The only thing that reels him in is being confronted by reality, and George, in the end, learns his lesson. He gets all humble again, Matt forgives him—it's like a marriage. The husband goes off and buys the water skis behind his wife's back, she gets all pissed off because it should have gone in the college education fund—that whole instant-gratification thing, as well as the power of television. You go to a new culture and find out what's in, and tap into it."

Just thinking about "Eyewitness News" amuses Gary Graham. "I did some things in there that I really did appreciate," he says. "Nobody could be more uncomfortable in front of a camera than Sikes. To sort of get into that point where you glaze over, which, of course, is exactly what you fight against being in front of the camera instead of doing what we always do, which is hide it, was pretty interesting. We had a lot of fun doing that episode. I was sorry that it didn't go as planned when the young Newcomer came in and was involved in this phone-sex thing.

"Originally, in the scene with her I was supposed to drop my pencil, these beautiful legs appear right in front of me, you follow my eyes all the way up her legs to finally look at her, and I'm kind of fumbling. They just watered that down and the whole effect was lost. I thought there should have been more of an overt attraction between the two, not just her doing veiled or slightly charming manipulations, but actually a real, sincere attraction between the two, which brings Sikes into his attraction/repulsion with the whole notion of having sex with an alien and dealing with Cathy later on."

TVS 16. "PARTNERS"

Original Airdate: February 12, 1990
Writers: David Garber and Bruce Kalish
Director: Stan Lathan
Guest Cast: Gilbert Lewis (Theo Miles)
Tom Byrd (Bud Anderson)
Crofton Hardester (Chester Charles)
Arthur Seidel (Desk Sergeant Rankin)
Robert Romanus (Zack Whelan)
Maria Ranger (Allison Wolfe)

George witnesses a powerful and well-connected mobster, Chester Charles, murder another man, thus ridding himself of the state's primary witness against him.

At a drug bust headed by Sikes's old mentor, Theo Miles, the cops locate a million dollars worth of "Jack," and George is asked to bring the drugs to the precinct, where they later turn up missing. George is accused of stealing it, becomes restricted to desk duty, and, later that night, his home is raided by a team of narcotics officers led by Miles and Sikes. The police find the missing drugs stashed behind a photograph of George and Susan, with the result that he is arrested, and his credibility as a witness against Chester Charles is destroyed. George claims he is a victim of a setup, a theory with which Sikes agrees wholeheartedly, and he soon discovers the truth about the drugs, Theo Miles's real allegiance, and the part that the mobster played in George's frame-up.

Now cleared of all charges, George goes with Susan to a pod-exchange area, where an incredible mixture of special effects and emotion takes place as the pod containing their child, Vessna, is transferred from Susan to George. (The male Newcomer then carries the child until birth, much as the male sea horse does.) Sikes, who has been chosen as Vessna's godfather, is in total awe of this strange and alien process.

NOTE: This episode establishes that both parents are biologically in sync with each other during pregnancy, each feeling what the other feels. A cute touch is watching George work out to a Jane Fonda video.

Commentary

AUTHOR'S RATING: ***

The most impressive aspect of "Partners" is the fact that Gary Graham and guest star Gilbert Lewis (as Theo Miles) almost instantly make the audience believe that these two have known each other for years. At the same time, a little bit more of Sikes's background is revealed, as well as an understanding of the man who influenced Sikes in becoming the police officer he is.

Although the framing of George Francisco is pretty obvious plot stuff—and it should be to just about everyone—it does provide the opportunity for Pierpoint to display some jealousy over Sikes's relationship with Theo. The latter's redemption at the end, again, is simplistic, though getting there provides Gary Graham with a splendid opportunity to convey the sense of betrayal he feels regarding Theo. His sense of loss is made tangible for the audience, once again proving that, emotionally, Matthew Sikes is definitely not a typical television cop.

The episode's real payoff occurs rightly at its climax, with the pod transfer from Susan to George. The special effects in this sequence are astounding by television standards, and the result is completely realistic.

There's a nice development in the relationship between Sikes and George, when the Franciscos want Sikes to be the godfather of their unborn child. As George explains it, they are trying to embrace certain human customs—though they found the book on the subject (*The Godfather* by Mario Puzo, 1970) a bit unsettling.

Behind-the-Scenes

"'Partners' was most memorable for the pod transfer," opines producer Andrew Schneider. "The network looked at the first cut of that and were freaked out. They thought people would turn off their TV sets. We made a few trims, but not much. Kenny [Johnson] really fought for this. He said, 'You guys are out of your mind. This is why people will watch the show. Even if some of them are a little aghast, they'll ask, "Hey, did you see *Alien Nation* last night?"' Again, not just to deal with another culture, but another physiology, and to see how they treat an aspect of their childbirth is great."

"The effects were feature quality and superb," enthuses story editor Steven Mitchell. "It was so interesting and so bizarre. It may be a little gross, but who cares? It's effective. That was another example of the show going to the edge successfully."

The series' other story editor, Craig Van Sickle, counters, "I guess when you have a gimmick like George being pregnant, you kind of get away with a weak story. I thought that if the 'A' part of the story had been better, you could have had great television instead of pretty darn good television. George's getting the pod is topnotch. The exchange might not be the easiest thing to watch, but if you can evoke a reaction from the audience, then you've gone above and beyond."

Producer Tom Chehak notes that this episode had "a lot of good character development between Sikes and the other cop. In the end, the baby is transferred to George, which was pretty amazing for television. We fought strong and hard and that scene was a result of everybody's effort. Fox fought us on this episode, tooth and nail. We won a lot of the battles and we lost a lot of them. This was one where we were victorious."

Gary Graham's pleasure from the episode comes from Sikes's relationship with and betrayal by Theo. "It was suddenly finding out that your dad was a drunk or your hero is a crook," he says. "It's disillusioning for Sikes. He's been kicked in the head before, many times, and this is a real bad one for him. The fact that this guy dies in his arms is the real bitterness of it. There's no restitution possible. It's over. He's not going to even pay his penance in life. That was powerful to do. One of my favorite scenes in the entire run of the series was where I confronted him outside the cop yard in the car."

It's noted that unlike many TV cops, Graham's Sikes isn't afraid to break down or come real close to being overwhelmed with his feelings during emotional moments, as is evident in "Partners."

"Guys do that," Graham points out. "I've seen that. I've seen it with cops. It's that horribly uncomfortable moment when manly men are hanging around and one of them is crumbling and you just don't know what to do. It is the most uncomfortable thing. People whose lives are at risk every day go through that. Then they jump back to the tough-guy thing just like that. Sikes is so fast to jump back there that he jumps back into the cave. The drama I think comes not with somebody crying or coming to tears, but fighting desperately not to; fighting to hold it in or suck it up, and anything that bleeds through is the pathos."

"Much of the episode was about trust, which has always been a very strong issue for George," says Eric Pierpoint. "He's pretty much built on trust; the way he sees the world and universe is one where he will trust blindly until proven otherwise. That's one of the qualities in the character when I was getting him together in the beginning and thinking of all the positive traits I could inject into him. Trust was certainly something that came up because it lays the groundwork to build so many other things. His trust of Matt and people doing right is paramount, but if you trust too much you can get yourself in trouble. I love the concept of him being wronged and having to deal with that psychologically.

"The transferring of the pod was another example of on-the-spot invention. At that time you're so deep into character that things happen you don't know are going to happen. In rehearsal you say, 'What is this ceremony and how do we do this?' Well, going in and having this wonderful kind of Garden-of-Eden setup to transfer the pod—how is it actually going to happen? Ken Johnson came down and the makeup people all came down and were trying to figure it out.

"'All right, you've got this thing over Susan's stomach, this sort of bowling ball inside there and this opening that sort of looks like the opening of a squid or something. And this thing sort of coming out...' It was so strange, because someone was underneath or just to the side of Michele [Scarabelli], working this radio-controlled mechanical tentacle. It's moving up, side to side, snake it out, it'll get pushed out. We're like, 'Oh, for God's sake, we can't watch this.' Many times when you're in the middle of acting and you're caught up in the pretend of it, the body and the mind sometimes don't really know [the difference].

"The best happens when you don't really know it's pretend, when you give up to it. You start to feel very emotional, very excited about this reality you're trying to portray. There were interesting things going on between Michele and me during the course of the year, insofar as being mates.... I was very much into feeling as a couple with her, especially at times like this when we were allowed to be that close.... In an ideal world, men and women would share the responsibility of children fifty-fifty, and that's what we're supposed to do in *Alien Nation*—try to break down the barriers and do that. Carrying the child turned out to be a fifty-fifty thing, and having the male actually do that, and having it be a totally natural process, is just too strange.

"As a male, you're saying, 'This is going to come out and attach itself to my nipple? Get out of here. I'm not doing this.' Then it comes out, and you say, 'Oh, *that's* what's supposed to happen?' You stuff it under your flap and eat part of the shell that broke, which reminds me of a German shepherd giving birth to her puppies and eating the placenta. I remember eating it and they said, 'Eat this one, it's chocolate; don't eat that one because it's bitter wax.' I got them confused and ended up stuffing this wax in my mouth and almost gagged on it during the scene. It was a very interesting show, because you've got two very strong things working at the same time and a split focus, yet both of them have great meaning. I enjoyed it."

TVS 17. "Real Men"

Original Airdate: February 19, 1990
Writers: Diane Frolov and Andrew Schneider
Director: John McPherson
Guest Cast: Debbie Barker (Karina)
Oscar Dillon (Body Builder)
Martin Garner (Sol Birnbaum)
Hank Garret (Marty Penn)
Joe Hoke (Cop)
M. C. Loree (Doctor)
A. D. Muylich (Victor Wendkos)
Neil Nash (Andrew)
Robert Neary (Dan Zinner)
Arthur Seidel (Rankin)
William Shockley (Nick Coletta)
Jeff Skier (Guest)
Patty Toy (Nurse)

The *macguffin* (a term invented by director Alfred Hitchcock to describe the pivotal plot device that triggers the action in a script) of "Real Men" involves the selling of Newcomer hormones, which are being used in humans as a new form of steroid that makes the body incredibly powerful, even though it often becomes fatal for the user. The true gist of the episode is that George is fully pregnant, going through everything that females go through when they're with child, from mood swings to swollen ankles.

Things tie together when Sikes and George trace the hormone thief, Dan Zinner, to a gymnasium and in the ensuing struggle Sikes is knocked out and George nearly killed, until his instincts take over and, in an effort to save his unborn child, he finally knocks out his opponent.

At that moment, however, George goes into premature labor and Sikes, practically in tears, is talked through delivering the child by George. Vessna is born perfectly healthy and, to keep her warm, Sikes takes off his shirt, drapes it over her, and, barechested, cuddles the infant, with George's aid, until help arrives.

NOTE: In this episode Sikes finally breaks down and tells Cathy that he likes her. Her reaction betrays the fact that the feeling is mutual.

Commentary

AUTHOR'S RATING: ***½

The steroid story line here is fairly interesting, once again providing the opportunity to use Tenctonese physiology as a means of enhancing human beings (as in episode TVS 02, "Fountain of Youth"), and opening up a debate on exactly what makes someone masculine. The question becomes a focal point for George, as he attempts to continue his functions as a police officer while dealing with his pregnancy. Eric Pierpoint deserves a lot of credit for making the audience believe without hesitation that he actually is pregnant. No easy task. There are moments, however, when he walks the fine line between hormone imbalance and a parody of pregnant women, usually landing on the side of the former.

Sikes finds himself torn in the middle, sympathetic to George's "condition" while adhering as much as possible to being a manly man. He's forced to go more with the latter when his old friend from Detroit, Nick Coletta, shows up and they relive old times. Later, though, his discomfort becomes obvious when Nick asks Cathy out on a date and he does absolutely *nothing* to stop it. Significant for the character is that he—*finally*—breaks down and admits that he has feelings for her.

As was the case in "Partners" (TVS 16), this episode truly comes to life at the climax when George goes into premature labor. The strength of the Graham-Pierpoint onscreen chemistry is at its best here when Sikes has no option but to help George give birth. There is not a single wrong step made in this sequence, giving every indication that we're watching an actual alien birth take place. The final moments of the scene, where the barechested Sikes huddles around George and the baby, is extremely powerful, and a testament to the abilities of these two actors. Just an incredible moment of television.

Behind-the-Scenes

"Most of the episode worked," notes story editor Steven Mitchell, "and that final shot proved that two men from different worlds could love each other. The birth makes it worth the price of admission."

Supervising producer Andrew Schneider explains, "We wanted to examine things in our culture that we take for granted about defining maleness and masculinity, and what better way to do that than through a pregnant male? So that for the humans, particularly a macho cop, it's very uncomfortable to have a pregnant male colleague. On another level, Sikes has this old friend, a macho partying guy, visiting him, who wants to date Cathy for sexual reasons, and Sikes isn't man enough to say 'I like this person, don't mess with her.' His turnaround at the end is that he's able to accept his feminine side, which is signified by his picking up knitting needles and telling Cathy that he likes her."

Co-producer Diane Frolov believes, "[The episode is] about accepting your feminine and masculine sides, and seeing that as a whole. If you deny one side, you really become a monster. You need both halves to make the whole person."

On the other hand, co-producer Tom Chehak wasn't as positive about this segment. "I had lots of battles over that one," he admits. "I felt it was almost an insult to women, that we were just mimicking the stereotype of a pregnant woman. I was very concerned with what we were saying there. Were we just making fun of women? The end scene where Sikes comes into touch with his feminine side was a real nice moment, but I was bothered by the tone of the whole piece. Generally, on our staff you bring something up, you fight for it, you say, 'I think we're making a big mistake,' and the majority rules. Kenny always says, 'Who's ever right wins.' The room said 'let's try it.' In the end, one of our writers, whose wife was pregnant, came in and said exactly what I feared, thinking that we were making fun of women. In general, I think the statement was right, but I was concerned with some of the attitudes."

"What can you say about 'Real Men'?" asks Eric Pierpoint rhetorically. "It was so much fun to do. I remember talking to a lot of women about their childbirth experience and how they felt, and I think you run the danger of any time a male pretends to be pregnant, the things that come out of your mouth end up being very campy, very cliché, and that's something we wanted to avoid. One of my all-time favorite scenes is when George is pissed off at Matt about something. He comes into the precinct, sits down, has an emotional moment, starts crying, starts arranging things on his desk and smacking something out of Matt's hand, and just carrying on. Matt is just sitting there, 'Here, have a Kleenex.'

"I love that. I love the innocence of him going through this body-building gymnasium and looking at all these men 'puffing up,' as he says, and he wonders what that has to do with being a man. To George, carrying a child is being a man. Once again, the confusion between the Tenctonese world and the human world, as well as issues of trust and partnership, come up. He questions himself about being a man because everyone around him is telling him what he's doing is not being a man.

"I used to live with someone who you never knew from one moment to the next who you were living with," he adds. "The emotional, hormonal stuff that was going on was an awesome experience. Whatever walked through that door would be something completely new and different. Some people, hormonally—dare I say, particularly women?—really have these enormous swings, but they think they're right on the money every time. That's what George was reacting to—just his body reacting to everything going on inside of him, and losing confidence in himself and despairing that maybe he wasn't a man, until he figured it out. I love the line when he's talking about Sylvester Stallone, 'That big, beefy fellow with the big gun who falls off cliffs and sews himself up—you think that's a man?' He figures out that's not really being a man."

The highlight of the episode for both Gary Graham and Eric Pierpoint is the final scene in which George goes into labor and Sikes has to help him give birth.

"A very tough scene," says Graham, "because we both agreed that we would commit to it. We didn't say anything about it, but we were both working real hard. Eric and I recognized the specialness of what this was, what it could be, and what it meant for each other. Of course, having subsequently gone through the birth of my own daughter, I learned that our instincts were absolutely right. It's such a life-or-death thing. People have been having babies since the beginning of time, but to be there when it's actually happening—you're struck so much with, 'Oh, my God, you could die. I could lose you.'

"The prospect of that, especially when I reached in and it

was breached [in the episode], was a real weird experience because this little thing was a remote-controlled device. Eric had this latex pouch, I'm actually on his stomach, moving around, and this thing is moving and it's all slimy. I truly had the sense that it was a baby and I was delivering it. It was nuts. When we brought it out, it looked cute. It was moving and all goobered-up. It was really a beautiful moment. We ad-libbed a bunch of stuff too, saying whatever popped out there. It was a neat thing to share with Eric."

Admittedly, some eyebrows were initially raised at the moment when Sikes removes his shirt and cuddles with George around the baby to keep it warm.

"The homophobes were probably diving for cover," admits Pierpoint. "I think some people thought it was too extreme, but from George it's absolutely natural for anything like that to happen and for him to express his thoughts and feelings about his friend. With Matt, there's got to be that reluctance yet that willingness to push forward."

Graham interjects, "I really appreciate the genius of our writers to have set up the notion of what is a man, what is manly, what are the attributes we cling to so desperately about manhood, and how can we shatter them? A real man, first of all, does what he has to do and does what is right at the time and dares to be sensitive and intimate. As my partner, the guy that I love, I'm helping him with his baby, and to keep the baby warm you don't even think about it, you just pull it close. So it's a further evolution of Sikes."

"I think that Matt truly sees in George a salvation for himself," Pierpoint concurs. "Or he senses something that George brings out in him which is a true friendship to believe in, despite the fact they're bickering half the time. Of course, Matt would be bickering with anybody half the time. And, again, you get involved in the pretend of it and some things come out that are very spontaneous that maybe were scripted and maybe weren't. George is huffing and puffing away, and Matt is holding his breath, and George says, 'Breathe, Matt.' I don't even know where that came from. Right at the end, when I look at the baby and say, for some reason, 'She has Susan's spots...'—that wasn't in the script. When you're deep in character like that is the only time that that can happen. That's the difference between doing the TV movies now and the series. It's sort of like watching Nimoy and Shatner on *Star Trek*—as they got older, the relationship was still there, but you could tell individually that each one of them seemed to have gone their separate ways."

TVS 18. "CROSSING THE LINE"

Original Airdate: February 26, 1990
Writers: Steven Long Mitchell and Craig Van Sickle
Director: Gwen Arner
Guest Cast: Robert Balderson (Wounded Officer)
Tobin Bell (Dr. Death)
Robert Alan Browne (Tool and Die Foreman)
Jenny Gago (Beatrice Zepeda)
Heather McComb (Cyndy)
Ivory Ocean (Dutchman)
Michelle Lamar Richards (Lois Allen)
Eva Von Widmann (Nurse)

Sikes's plans for going on a Hawaiian vacation are put on hold when the precinct gets a report of a serial killer on the loose, whose m.o. seems to fit a murder suspect Sikes had been after a full decade earlier.

Through flashbacks, we learn that as a uniformed cop Sikes came up against Dr. Death, who had taken a hostage and ordered him to throw aside his gun or else the good doctor would kill the young woman. Believing him, Sikes did what he was told, but the girl was killed by the doctor anyway and Sikes was wounded. Living with the pain ever since, now he has an opportunity to even the score, no matter what the cost, whether it be the reporter, Burns, who is being manipulated by the killer, or even George.

NOTE: When taking in tobacco, the Tenctonese body goes through a series of twitches and the individual begins to stutter.

Commentary

AUTHOR'S RATING: ***

As effective an episode as "Crossing the Line" is, its story line could have taken place on just about any other cop show. There is virtually nothing featured here that impacts on the Tenctonese, other than the fact that George is trying to do what he can for his partner.

The story places emphasis on an indictment of journalism taken too far when a reporter ends up playing an active role in creating the news he's then covering. Jeff Doucette does a nice job in his meatiest turn as the reporter, Burns. Ironically, this represents his most substantial exposure on the series—and it occurs *after* he was removed from the series' opening credits. Then, too, Tobin Bell is effective—albeit a bit overly melodramatic—as Dr. Death.

What makes this episode special is Gary Graham's portrayal of Sikes, providing yet another guided tour of the character's personal hells and impressively allowing the character's obsession over the good doctor to wear him down, both physically and emotionally.

Behind-the-Scenes

"The network asked for a strong human story to help develop Sikes," says story editor Craig Van Sickle. "It was written under the confines of what the network wanted, because we really didn't want to do a story like 'Takeover,' where there wasn't any emotion involved. We tried to bring it to the level of 'Why is Sikes so concerned about this?' For what it was on that level, it was very successful."

Co-story editor Steven Mitchell adds, "It could have been on any show. You didn't need the aliens there, but it was something the network asked for. Basically they had just gotten a fresh batch of audience research, and what usually happens then is that they throw themselves into a panic and say, 'Our research shows that Matt Sikes is underdeveloped and we need to give him more emotional impact.' That's basically what that whole thing was about. It turned out very well, but it would have been nice to have a little more alien aspects to it."

Producer Andrew Schneider notes, "We wanted to examine the rights of a free press in our society. Does the press create the news? What is its responsibility? I think the strongest parts of the show were the scenes between Sikes and the reporter, dealing with his rights and how they conflicted with those of the police and people."

Eric Pierpoint's only comment regarding the segment is how effectively Gary Graham portrays Sikes's obsession. "He was just so raw in that episode," he says. "I think it's one of his best episodes."

"I love that episode," enthuses Graham. "Early on, right after the pilot, we all got together and the actors were asked for input as to what little scenarios we'd like to see; little things our characters could do. The writers compiled it all and throughout the season little bits and pieces of those would pop up in the episodes. One of my chief contributions was a little scenario that basically had Sikes going into deep, deep cover. In fact, becoming a renegade cop to catch a killer. My scenario was a little different, but it was basically the gist of 'Crossing the Line,' because I wanted to go outside and be a cop who needed to come in, a cop who was driven and obsessed by this thing. My attitude in the episode was so brittle and sharp and fierce. It's so aberrant, but it worked out perfect because this guy is really going off here. George, being as intuitive as he is, finally figures it out that I didn't go to Hawaii and tracks me down. I just loved it. Additionally, Gwen Arner directed it—no wonder I love it."

Interestingly, much of the Burns part of the story—and his involvement with the episode's killer—is similar to Stephen Lang's reporter and what he goes through with a serial killer in the feature film *Manhunter* (1986), based on the novel *Red Dragon* (and prequel to 1991's *The Silence of the Lambs*). Of Burns, Graham says, "Burns was like a gnat that I was always swatting away. We kind of came up with funny little things that I was fond of, and I was sorry that I never had a chance to sort of warm up with him. Maybe in a weird, strange situation sharing beers and opening up and then catching myself, 'What am I telling *you* this for?' I'm sorry we never got to that. In this episode he shows up at a crime scene. I have a few words with him, and say, 'What's this?' He looks down and I tweak his nose. 'Real mature, Sikes.' We were always making up little things like that. He sort of brought out the fifth-grade idiot in me. Jeff Doucette is a funny guy."

TVS 19. "Rebirth"

Original Airdate: March 12, 1990
Writer: Tom Chehak

Director: Tom Chehak
Guest Cast: Brian Thompson (Peter Rabbit)
Ellen Wheeler (Okno)
John Sudol (Sikes's Father)
Ryan Cash (Young Sikes)
Raffi Diblasio (Billy Boardman)

George and Sikes attempt to capture robbery suspect Peter Rabbit, who takes from the rich and gives to the poor. As they close in on him, Rabbit slams Sikes into a high-voltage fence. George rushes him to the hospital where he is reported to have died, but Rabbit, who belongs to a Tenctonese religious sect called Luibof, uses mystic crystals to bring Sikes back to life.

Sikes spends the rest of the episode seeking some answers and, in the process, comes to grips with his past, which includes his relationship with his father who, it turns out, has spent two decades in a coma.

NOTE: Guest star Brian Thompson (Peter Rabbit) is best known these days to genre fans for his recurring role as the alien bounty hunter on Fox's *The X-Files* (1993–).

Commentary

AUTHOR'S RATING: ****

Once certain confusing, metaphysical aspects of this episode are accepted, this segment can be relished for the acting skills of both Gary Graham and Eric Pierpoint, in this particular case the former for drama and the latter for humor.

This trip into Sikes's past is extremely effective, illuminating his relationship with his father and, through the character's guilt, providing insight into his current personality. The fact that his father is still alive (somewhat implausibly) but nonetheless out of reach, is incredibly frustrating and Matt's pain is obvious. His desperation to apprehend the Newcomer, Peter Rabbit, who he believes resurrected him in order to heal his father, feels extremely *real* and his disappointment at the end completely understandable. Incidentally, Sikes's death works very well, portraying the possibility of sudden death that a cop faces daily as a part of the normal routine.

In turn, Eric Pierpoint manages to bring us back to Neil Simon territory once again, as he and Graham do their take on *The Odd Couple* when George asks him for some tips on how to coach Emily's Little League team. These scenes are some of George's liveliest and most adorable moments, and Sikes's frustration with him has the greasy fingerprints of Oscar Madison all over it.

Behind-the-Scenes

"That was a long battle," episode writer-director Tom Chehak details. "What I wanted to do was a metaphysical show about a guy in search of his roots and who he is. I wanted to do a story about Jesus Christ, really, and how people have conceived their life and their Lord. That was my original conception. The original show began with Sikes getting shot and rushed to the emergency ward, where he is pronounced dead. It was a Christmas show, and it turns out that his [Sikes's] father [attempted to] kill himself the night before Christmas. [Instead, he hadn't died but, thereafter, existed in a coma.] Sikes [now] has this dark memory of Christmas.... In the very last scene, which is the same as the first scene, he's coming into the emergency ward, but instead of Sikes dying on the table, the doctor comes out and says to George, 'It looks like he's going to survive. It's going to be the miracle of Christmas after all,' and he pulls through. So the whole show took place in one metaphysical moment of life and death.

"Of course, the network didn't understand metaphysics, nor did they feel our audience could," he continues. "As far as they were concerned, the events couldn't happen in a flash of a moment like that. But I still really loved the idea of Sikes dying and coming back, so I came up with the idea of these crystals and Sikes searching for the healer who brought him back to life, hence the connection with his father, and we got that whole backstory there. It's a show that's important to me, because I made my directorial debut on it and wrote it, but it's a show that fired on five of its six cylinders. I thought it was an interesting show, and the kind of vein we should have done more of. When you're writing science fiction, you like to play with the medium as much as you can, but the networks don't want you to do that."

Story editor Steven Mitchell adds, "Why the network was scared of Tom's original idea, I don't know. It was compromised into something that wasn't as good as it could have been, which was always my disappointment. It's one thing when you say, 'We can build the Empire State Building,' and you end up with townhouses, but you keep the Empire State Building in mind, so even if those townhouses are nice, it's not the same thing."

"I think you have to commend the episode for the ambition that was behind it," enthuses co-story editor Craig Van Sickle. "It tried to do more in an hour of TV than most people care to think about. So although not totally successful on every level, there's a lot of nice things in there. It gets an A+ for effort, that's for sure. I think Tom's direction, especially for a first episode, was splendid."

Eric Pierpoint notes, "You've got a couple of things going on here. You've got Sikes being forced to look back at his unhappy childhood. Then there's the responsibility that rests on George's shoulders, comically, to be the coach of Emily's

Little League team. He's so excited because this supersedes everything. He has gone about studying in the library everything there is about baseball and coaching, but his only knowledge is reading about it. He doesn't know how to play the game. He can tell you the batting pose or fielding pose of all the players on the bubble-gum cards, but he doesn't know how to play. It was so much fun to do because we got to a baseball field. George takes off, runs around the diamond and wants to do his Pete Rose slide, and ends up ten feet short, practically taking off for the slide from second base into third. 'I came up a little short, but how was my form?' he asks as he goes back to Matt, who's just moaning and complaining when George begs him to help him.

"Then it gets into all kinds of comic possibilities—how many ways can he miss the ball? With something like that, it's fun because if you can still believe it well enough, you can be a clown as an actor as long as you're consistent with the character trying so hard. The things that stuck out in that are, of course, the comedy and the seemingly healthy home life of George versus the kind of lost soul that Matt is and all of the stuff he's going through with his family. There is such a contrast between these two beings. In spite of all the hardships he's had, George is the eternal optimist and Matt is the pessimist. George is getting better by growing up and associating and assimilating the stuff around him. I'm probably going to go to my grave thinking, 'Well, at least I got one really great character to do in my lifetime.' One of those characters that kind of has a life of its own."

Gary Graham laughs about the story line: "Matt's father's been in a coma for twenty years? Who's paying for that? Are taxpayers paying for this life support? Why didn't they pull the plug a long time ago? Seriously, I thought it was a great episode. Tom Chehak wrote and directed. He and I both share a strong

Christian faith. We had Sikes as sort of a recovering Catholic and, in his being awestruck in coming back to life when all hope was lost, he saw the chance of maybe his dad being brought back and his being given the opportunity to make amends and deal with the guilt he's been carrying for so long....

"One of the most powerful moments in the episode," he continues, "is when Sikes tries to hold it together in the hospital. He's there with George in the hallway and George says, 'Go and talk to your father.' When I entered the room to talk to dad, what I felt happening at the time, as I recall, was that all pretense was dropped. I really felt reverted to that little boy tiptoeing in to say 'I'm sorry' to daddy. It was really a moving moment for me. Every kid wants approval from daddy. Everything that Sikes has done the last twenty years has been a factor of knowing that, unless his dad comes out of the coma, he can never regain that approval. It's lost. There's a special place in my heart for Tom Chehak for doing that episode. It's really a gift when a guy writes a part that is so rich for you and then he directs it."

TVS 20. "GIMME, GIMME"

Original Airdate: April 9, 1990
Writers: Andrew Schneider and Diane Frolov
Director: David Carson
Guest Cast: Beege Barkette (EPA Official)
Kim Braden (Marilyn Houston)
Joseph Cali (Lee Smith)
Alan Fudge (Sleepy Phil)
Beverly Leech (Rita Allen-Poe)
Bob Minor (Cop)
Lance E. Nichols (Delivery Man)
Michelle Lamar Richards (Lois Allen)

David Selburg (Edgar Allen-Poe)
Armin Shimerman (Cyril Roman)
Michael Zand (Mr. Lias)

Nu-Knit is a stain-free, nearly impervious Tenctonese fabric about to be manufactured on Earth, and the company behind the product is seeking investors. George and Susan decide to take a risk and invest $10,000, believing that they will earn ten times their money.

Suddenly, Nu-Knit's developer, Edgar Allen-Poe, is murdered by someone who has filled the water in his swimming pool with sea salt. While chasing down suspects, Sikes and George learn that the company's treasurer, Cyril Roman, has been buying up stock under assumed names so that he can gain control of the firm. Additionally, they uncover that Allen-Poe was killed because the manufacturing of Nu-Knit resulted in toxic waste, a fact he was going to reveal, thus destroying the company's credibility with the public.

Meanwhile, when Albert Einstein wins a lottery he buys Sikes the automobile that Matt has spent years dreaming about, but Sikes learns, ultimately, that having is not so pleasing a thing as wanting.

NOTE: Armin Shimerman, who portrays Roman, is well-known by sci-fi fans for his characterizations of Paskal in *Beauty and the Beast* (1987–90) and the Ferengi barkeep, Quark, in *Star Trek: Deep Space Nine* (1993–).

Commentary

AUTHOR'S RATING: **½

This episode attempts a plethora of social commentary, from protecting the environment and the horrors of sweat shops to discovering that the things we want are never what they are expected to be. With so many tangents to explore, however, the segment is only moderately successful. Great humor is generated by Sikes and his car, and the Franciscos spending the returns on their investment practically before they've handed over their money. The "mystery" itself, as presented in this installment, doesn't work nearly as well. Buck's activism quickly grows annoying, particularly as he's pressured by his teacher, Marilyn Houston, in what turns out to be a setup for the subsequent season cliffhanger. It proves to be not a bad offering, but certainly not up to the series' best creative efforts.

Behind-the-Scenes

"We wanted to do an ecological show," notes supervising producer Andrew Schneider. "The basic theme is that things that we want, which we think improve the quality of life, in fact destroy the quality of life. Sikes's metaphor was this car he had dreamt about, which turned out to be a burden that was ruining his life. On a larger level, there was this wonder fabric, the creation of which could destroy the Earth. Again, we wanted to do kind of a lighter episode, a whodunit. I'm very fond of that one."

Co-story editor Craig Van Sickle disagrees. "Some nice elements, but much lighter than our personal view of the show had been. We tended to go a little darker. I think it was one of the first episodes that started to get real fluffy, which set alarm bells off in my mind. I think some of the comedy is good, but I can't say it's one of my favorites."

"Obviously," says the other story editor, Steven Mitchell, "you could see that Andy and Diane's stuff was, for the most part, lighter. Our stuff was a little bit darker and Tom's fell in the middle. On the one hand, I think that was one of the strengths of *Alien Nation.* When you tuned in, you weren't sure what you were going to see. Sort of what they did on *Magnum, P. I.* [1980–88]. You didn't know if they were going to have an intense show, a light show, a straight P.I. show. It's too bad we didn't get to go on with that creative team."

Producer Tom Chehak points out, "Originally, it was a very dark show conceived by Diane. These people at the factory were Newcomers who ate the dead on the ship to get rid of the waste. Everybody hated them because they were such vulgar, awful people. Now they were eating all of the garbage on this planet to get rid of the waste. It would have been a wonderful episode, but we got beat up with 'You can't do that, you can't do this.' Ultimately the idea was totally diluted. Diane loved the idea of the toxicity and how we're destroying our planet, so she kept that thread and everything else got diluted. I think once you dilute it, once the studio or the network—whoever's involved—starts diluting the concept, you lose the real fire of that story. It was originally very fascinating. If the censors, the networks, and all that stuff had just gone away, we could have done some really interesting things."

It should be noted here that the darker elements of this story eventually would be resurrected in the fourth *Alien Nation* TV movie, *The Enemy Within*.

"I loved watching that one again," laughs Gary Graham. "I'd forgotten how funny we all were. I also like the theme of the show—we spend so much time trying to get *things* that we kind of lose track of just how much they cost. They all end up costing more than you anticipate—George's investment and Sikes's car. The price, the headache, the hassle, time commitment, how it colors your attitude, changes your mood, your relationship with people. Things start to become more important than people. Again, *Alien Nation* is walking the tightrope between drama and comedy, such that it's seamless. I'd forgotten how well the cast, the writers, and the directors all worked together to do real funny comedy that is sometimes so dark that you don't even realize it's funny until you find yourself laughing about it later."

"Let's face it, there's no such thing as the easy way," says Eric Pierpoint. "It just doesn't happen. I learned that from my own financial investments that didn't kill me, but certainly damaged me. So here George and Susan invest the whole wad in something totally ridiculous. The designer colors were really fun, because the Tenctonese always think the gaudiest colors are really, really pretty. George wandering around with this ugly vest on was just amazing. Pretty much a middle-of-the-road episode."

TVS 21. "THE TOUCH"

Original Airdate: April 16, 1990
Writers: Steven Long Mitchell and Craig Van Sickle
Director: Harry Longstreet
Guest Cast: Jenny Gago (Beatrice Zapeda)
Barbara Bush (Lorraine Clark)
Jonathan Brandis (Andy Day/Andron)
Mitchell Allen (Andron, age seven)
Mike Preston (Rigac)
Ella Day (Dorothy Fielding)
Martin La Platney (Troy)
Doug Ballard (Mr. Eugene)
Margaret Howell (Andron's Mother)

Cathy encounters Andron, a youth she had befriended and loved on the slave ship but who is now cold and distant towards her. Enlisting the help of Sikes and George, she learns that Andron has become the victim of the Overseers who, as the Nazis did via Project Odessa, are trying to train a new generation of "chosen ones" to one day rule over the supposedly "inferior" race.

To accomplish this goal, they take charge of the children during their early developmental years and deny them love by placing metallic bands over their temples. As the Tenctonese express much of their love through the touching of their temples, this cruel method turns the youngsters into unfeeling machines. Cathy is determined to free the youth from this mental trap, even if she has to resort to kidnapping him, and, while Sikes and George want to help her, they are bound by the law to stop her efforts.

NOTE: Guest star Jonathan Brandis, who portrays Andron, is probably best known to genre fans for his costarring role on the 1990s Steven Spielberg-produced TV series *seaQuest DSV* (1993-96).

Commentary

AUTHOR'S RATING: ***

Gary Graham and Eric Pierpoint seem more like guest stars in this installment, having little more to do than say things like "Cathy, don't do this", "Tell us where the boy is, Cathy", and so on. Nevertheless, "The Touch" is an extremely effective episode. Not only does it allow Terri Treas to score in her strongest portrayal of Cathy yet, but it also rapidly establishes the feeling of a true relationship between her and Jonathan Brandis's Andron. She conveys Cathy's love for this boy powerfully, as well as showing her frustrations at not being able to reach him emotionally for much of the episode.

What works best about the show, however, is, once again, the insight it offers about the Tenctonese, essentially giving a guided tour of the creation of the Overseers, providing succinct lessons on how they would turn what could be a loving child into a cold-hearted monster. There is something very unsettling about the knowledge that the Overseers are preparing the next generation of their kind. Great stuff!

Behind-the-Scenes

"That was a little atypical to what Steve and I wrote," explains co-story editor Craig Van Sickle. "Although there's an edge to it, without a doubt, we also delved into something of a 'message'. I think we were able to do that on an entertaining and intriguing level. The reaction we've gotten from people in the child-abuse field is really quite positive. The actress, Terri Treas, is very involved with that, and we talked to her about the story. Every show about child abuse is always done in a way that the dad comes home with the T-shirt on, he's been drinking, and the belt comes off his pants. It's tough to watch and you don't always absorb what's going on."

His fellow story editor, Steven Mitchell, interjects, "What we try to do is not let the audience know what they are watching until it's 'too late.' Eventually you realize that this thing was about love, and not Hitler youth. The groundswell we got in response was surprising. It seems to have had a real positive effect, and one that we didn't even know until after it aired."

Craig adds, "'The Touch' is one of the most alien of all the episodes. It has them dealing with something in a new venue on Earth. I think the idea of creating a generation of Overseers is done in a way that our audience can relate to without really knowing why. Our hope was that at the end of that they would have absorbed something without sitting there and saying, 'Boy, they really handled child abuse well,' not really having a handle on what it was. I think from the feedback we've gotten, we succeeded."

"A very sweet show," says producer Tom Chehak. "We wanted to do a show with Cathy and wanted to explore her past a little bit. I think basically the script was better than the final execution of it. It fired on maybe three cylinders."

TVS 22. "GREEN EYES"

Original Airdate: April 23, 1990
Writers: Diane Frolov and Andrew Schneider
Director: Tom Chehak
Guest Cast: Jenny Gago (Beatrice Zapeda)
Barbara Bush (Lorraine Clark)
Michelle Lamar Richards (Dr. Lois Allen)
Lee Bryant (Phyllis Bryant)
Kim Braden (Marilyn Houston)
Jaskell V. Anderson III (Principal Fisher)
John Calvin (Rick Parris)
Geoffrey Bryant (Michael Bukowski)
Thomas Knickerbocker (Judge Kaiser)
Thom Zimerele (Joshua Tree)
Andras Jones (Noah Ramsey)
Geoff Pierson (Dr. Bogg)

Cliffhangers like you wouldn't believe!

Sikes and Cathy share their first kiss and it badly frightens him, so he retreats to the arms of human social worker Lorraine Clark. By the time he sees the light, Cathy has decided that she can't be human for him and, until Sikes accepts her for what she is (an alien), they can have no future together.

The ever-rebellious Buck becomes fascinated with his American history teacher and discovers that the two of them have a lot in common, which leads to their inter-species affair.

George passes the exam for grade-level Detective-Two and is now, technically, Sikes's superior, something that George never lets Matt forget. It starts off as good-natured joking, changes to George giving Sikes subservient assignments, and comes down to his pulling rank, resulting in Sikes announcing that he's putting in for a new partner.

All of these actions flesh out the main plot in which the Purists have developed a bacteria that kills Newcomers, and hope that, within two weeks, they'll have produced enough to wipe out the entire Tenctonese community. At episode's end, Susan and Emily Francisco are infected, with Cathy delivering the news to a stunned Sikes.

Commentary

AUTHOR'S RATING: ***½

This episode proved to be an overloaded season finale and cliffhanger that worked for the most part, though it could have jettisoned Buck's affair without missing a beat (indeed, this plot line was dropped years later in the 1994 cliffhanger-resolving TV movie *Dark Horizon*). What is extremely effective about the show, however, are the relationships between Sikes and Cathy, and Sikes and George.

It is extremely frustrating—though admittedly realistic—to see Sikes and Cathy share their first kiss, and for him to back away, out of fear, from their potential relationship. This result is particularly poignant after all she has done to be "human" for him. Her final resolution, to end their potential future together, is a wrenching decision but an honest one. Gary Graham and Terri Treas deserve a lot of credit for making these characters real to the viewer and true to their basic natures.

The tension between George and Sikes over his Detective-Two status starts off humorously, but takes on a decidedly darker spin as George regards the promotion *far* too seriously. The slap-fight between them at episode's end is hysterical. There is also real tension generated in the Purists' creation of an ultimate weapon (in the form of a virus) to be used against the Tenctonese. It's a frightening development, the impact of which might have been wide-reaching in terms of the series—if not for the fact that it would take four years for the audience to find out what happened.

All in all, this episode was an effective way to end the show's first—and ultimately only—TV season.

Behind-the-Scenes

Producer Tom Chehak admits, "That was a show that tried to accomplish an awful lot. I was not there for the conception of the show; it was being conceived while I was directing 'Rebirth' [TVS 19], which is why they didn't want me to direct as much as I wanted, because I would be thrown out of the loop. It was really Diane and Andy. They wanted a cliffhanger episode. I think they tried too much. We didn't need the Buck story, for instance, and I don't think we needed a lot of the stuff we were doing. But, again, by the time I got involved I couldn't make any major changes, and we went with it."

Story editor Craig Van Sickle says, "I don't know what really happened, but I don't think it was anybody's fault. I think we got into a thing again with the network's interference that it had to be a certain way. I also think that in some ways everyone had their eyes towards the next fall, which was dictating what we did at the end of this episode."

"It was a forced cliffhanger," co-story editor Steven Mitchell emphasizes, "and quite frankly I don't think it did the show justice. It should have been a bigger show, where we had more emotional impact. What happened, as had happened in the past, is that we started with a decent idea and it kind of got watered down along the way, to the point where it's like, 'Are Buck and his teacher going to get together?' Who cares? We know all of our principles aren't going to be killed, so big deal they went to the hospital. We know they'll be fine. We had different ideas completely. It just kind of lays there and doesn't do anything special.

"What we were going to do in 'The Touch' was that the little boy they were going to make an Overseer was going to be given a special spot on the back of his head. At the end of that episode we were going to see that George's baby had the same spot, which was a sign that she was destined to be an Overseer. The next episode would be the baby being kidnapped, George finding out where she was—along with some emotional stuff concerning Sikes—and a totally different thing focusing on our people, and not this grand 'let's kill them all' plot."

"I think Steve touched on the biggest problem," states Van Sickle. "It was a threat 'out there,' as opposed to one focusing on George and the family of characters. It got so 'out there' and big, a lot like 'Contact.' That's its biggest problem."

Mitchell adds, "The scripts were being written for next year, and the first episode was cluttered again because you had to wrap up all the stories. So the new stories wouldn't have started until show three, because there were all those stories to wrap up. That was indicative of the problems of that episode."

Gary Graham points out that the Sci-Fi Channel recently ran a marathon of science-fiction cliffhangers, and included this *Alien Nation* episode. "My reaction," he smiles, "was that we don't qualify because we were able to resolve our cliffhanger—it just took us four years. I thought 'Green Eyes' was great. I loved the notion of Sikes feeling a little weird about dating an alien and wondering why he wasn't dating a human female, even though he still had the hots for Cathy and the other woman was just an excuse for him to feel normal and not feel as though he had a problem. As you know, Sikes had a lot of problems in general, and we found out about a new one in each episode. I would tell the writers, 'Each new script, I look to see what new problem Matt is dealing with.'"

The Purist angle of the story line intrigued Eric Pierpoint. "It's interesting to play someone who's the object of prejudice," he says. "It's interesting to then look at other races with that in mind. We were having to constantly do this, put ourselves in the position of imagining that you were the object of racism and that anything you did wasn't good enough, based on the fact that you have a big, spotty head. I have a lot of black friends, especially this one guy in particular who lives in the same condominium complex I used to live in. He and his wife came over for dinner and we were talking, and while I was looking at him I thought, 'What would it be like? How horrible a thing is it to be sitting there and have the history of so many people looking at you, fearing you, despising you simply because you've got a different skin-color? Or feeling that you're a second-class citizen because of this, and having to overcome it. As a white man, I can only imagine. You've got to feel for them because it's just numbing that this stuff can happen. And it exists all over the place; it hasn't gone away. It can only go away in areas of your own life.

"In terms of the Purist thing, in a sense Matt is in the middle of seeing members of his own race behave in a despicable way," he continues. "As much as George hates this, he has to walk into Nazi headquarters, into the land of hate, and face down some Purists and say, 'If you ever do this, I'll kill you.' You could see their hatred and you could see George's willingness to go gun-crazy and kill them all. The absolute reactionary hate from a dignified man. A hate that comes out of defending his dignity and thinking that that kind of prejudice is pure evil. I like that about the character, where he has such a moral implant in him that you can't miss it. He knows what he likes and what he doesn't. He's an innately moral person, which is why in 'Red Room' they could never bring him around. It's very heroic. There's not a lot of gray area."

Which is not to say that both he and Graham didn't enjoy the fight between Sikes and George at the episode's conclusion.

"Like little boys," laughs Pierpoint. "That's gleeful. That was a spontaneous thing, practically an improv, turning what was written into the Three Stooges. Kenny used to tell me that at dailies they would howl when we got into that shit. To me, that's the heart of the show. You go from one extreme to another in two minutes and end up saving each other. That's the show that was so much fun. Gary calls me up all the time and says, 'I was watching one of the episodes the other night. God, that was so much fun. Do you remember when we...' Just a tremendous experience."

Graham adds that the shooting of that fight was "a classic day. We had so much fun doing a little slapstick. It was like two little kids who are pushing each other, 'Stop it.' 'No, you stop it.' 'No, *you* stop it,' and pretty soon you're slap-fighting. I was just splitting a gut that day. I know we did it very seriously, but believe me, when they yelled 'cut' we were down there, locked in fierce battle, just laughing our heads off."

As the episode credits for "Green Eyes" began rolling on April 23, 1990, fans of *Alien Nation* had no idea that it would take four years for that segment's various cliff-hanging story lines finally to be resolved.

CANCELATION

In the summer of 1990, the cast and crew of *Alien Nation* sat back with pride, feeling that they had accomplished something that few TV programs of the era could claim: they had challenged the television audience.

As the series concluded its first season with a cliffhanger, the staff already had begun laying out plans for year two, taking the characters and the tapestry of *Alien Nation* into even bolder plot directions. The first production step, naturally, would be to fly the show's main cast to New York from California to participate in Fox Broadcasting's annual presentation for the various advertising agencies. Then, at literally the last moment, the word came out from the studio: the series had been canceled.

"I was just in disbelief," admits costar Gary Graham. "All the indications that had ever been given were not only would the show be renewed, but they were completely behind us. They were having me in to Fox to do this taped answer-your-fan-mail stuff. They booked us flights to New York, Chicago, and Detroit to do the affiliate meetings. Then they said, 'Wait a minute, maybe not. Maybe half-hour sitcoms are the way to go. Let's ax the dramas."

Eric Pierpoint, the other lead actor of *Alien Nation*, admits to being as shocked as anyone by the turn of events. "After the success of *The Simpsons* [1989–], FBC [Fox Broadcasting Corporation], I'm sure, said, 'How many people are willing to switch off from UHF to VHF because of this cartoon?' I think it resulted in the creative decision to cancel the one-hour dramas and come back with a lot of half-hour comedies.... I always withhold a little bit of myself, because I know in this business you can be shocked, period....

"We were all upset about it and felt that it was premature," he continues. "We were just getting started. There's a difference between sweating it out if you're on a show that's mediocre versus sweating it out on a show that you feel is entertaining and has some value. A lot of the Fox executives would say, 'We think your show has the most potential of all our shows.' We were told, 'You're on every tentative schedule we've figured out so far.' I didn't know who to believe and who not to believe. All I know is that the result is that they went another way. They were gambling."

Series' supervising producer Andrew Schneider insists, "This wasn't just another TV show. This was very dear to us, and the show's cancelation was a terrible blow. We fought tooth and nail to get it resurrected at the time and were really devastated when we couldn't find some other venue for it. We thought our numbers were good enough, coupled with the tremendous critical acclaim we had received. It's like someone taking your baby away, or someone in your family dying."

Producer Tom Chehak feels, "I think it all boiled down to the higher-ups at Fox not liking the show. Everything we heard was that we would be picked up, but I was not shocked only in the sense that I'm not shocked by anything that happens in this town anymore. I think the show accomplished a great deal for television. You can address issues and do things in a different form. That's the only reason I was so disappointed to see something like that go. You're losing, number one, a real interesting show and a science fiction show that doesn't take itself as seriously as *Star Trek*, and isn't as silly as *The Jetsons*. We're somewhere in between. *Alien Nation* was a great gig, and I was sorry to see it go."

Story editor Steven Mitchell adds, "I was pretty astonished by the cancelation. There was no *reason* for it. We knew it was the favorite show of the affiliates and that it sold the products that were being advertised. For those reasons alone, I couldn't see Fox taking it off the air."

Craig Van Sickle, Mitchell's writing partner, considers all that transpired and summed up his opinion in one sentence: "You never know what happens behind closed corporate doors."

Executive producer Ken Johnson had been through cancelation and creative differences before in the TV business. He was the guy who launched *"V"* on NBC, and then walked away from the franchise when the network wanted a cheaper version for the sequel.

"It's happened to me a few times," relates Johnson. "*'V'* I had enormous passion for, and still to this day feel that they really killed the golden goose there. They had an opportunity to do such wonderful stuff, which they blew. I pointed that out to Fox Broadcasting this time, that they were doing the same thing. But it's very hard sometimes to get across to people, because they think you're trying to be self-serving and keep yourself on the air. They don't realize that somehow I manage to keep feeding my family every week, with or without them."

Johnson's frustration stems from the fact that *Alien Nation* was a product that he knew was high-quality and felt that it was being treated badly by the network. "I was privileged to pick up the Viewers for Quality Television Founders Award for the show," he says. "It was presented to us at the ceremony where they honored all the people the organization selects for trying to put forward quality on television. We were in the good company of Candice Bergen, Dana Delaney, and Scott Bakula, and my pal Steven Bochco was the keynote speaker. It was very rewarding. Also, I picked up another award from the Community Relations Conference of Southern California, which is an organization devoted to fostering better understanding between interracial people in Los Angeles. That was really terrific, because *Alien Nation* was all about community relations. It's nice to do a show that you care about, that you feel can make some sort of contribution to society. That's what I've tried to do in all my work, and certainly what *Alien Nation* was all about and continues to be."

Pierpoint admits that there was another, more selfish aspect of his disappointment: he would have to leave George Francisco behind him.

"The immediate feeling was the loss of the character," he admits. "That's the main thing that hit me. I thought, 'My God, I'm not going to be able to play this character anymore,' and that upset me. I was pretty devastated when I realized that George Francisco would no longer be a part of my life as an actor. I was messed up after that. Then I started hearing all kinds of things. I started to hear organizations for quality programming, critics, and the public, and there was this outcry, according to Fox. They were besieged from all angles. 'Why are you doing this? Why are you canceling *Alien Nation*?' And the response was, 'Well, it's too expensive for the ratings it gets.'

"It's tough to argue their point of view. It's a money thing, and Hollywood is always a money thing. They don't really let shows grow like they used to with *St. Elsewhere* [1982–88], *Hill Street Blues* [1981–87], or *Cheers* [1982–93]. We were lucky to get one year. If nothing else, at least I feel good that I was involved with something that people appreciated on a level other than just performance. It was much more meaningful and more powerful than that. *That* nobody can take away. We made a difference."

Graham points out that he's objective enough to separate his own involvement with the show to say that it is still one of his favorite series.

"I just love to watch it and can actually separate myself from it," he says. "I was a great fan as an observer, not just a participant. I loved what the show had to say, I loved the way it was said, the combination of chemistries we ended up with. We fell together and everyone kind of said, 'What if I do this?', 'Hey, that gives me an idea. Why don't I do that?', 'You lean this way, I'll walk that way, we'll talk this way,' and we all put it together, working hard and having fun doing so. Some shows, it's time to leave them. They've had their heyday and it's time to do the farewell episode, but we all felt very strongly that this show's time had not come yet. There were too many untold stories."

Johnson and company probably had the last laugh, appropriately enough. In the 1990–91 TV season, Fox's Monday night schedule completely fell apart, the network having no choice but to replace *21 Jump Street* and *Alien Nation* with two-hour movies. Among the shows debuting that year were such forgettable sitcom fare as *Get a Life, Good Grief, Babes* (described as *Roseanne* times three), *Totally Hidden Video*, and *Haywire*.

"We were pretty infuriated," says Johnson, "and I think most of the people at Fox felt the same way from the beginning. Certainly it's been underlined now because of what happened to them on Mondays the following season. It's just astonishing. They never cease to amaze me over there. But I think they all had a dose of cold water, because the 1990 season just did not materialize the way they had expected it to. I think they probably saw that the cancelation of the show was a mistake, that it was a signature show and that all the new one-hours they've put on have not done as well as we did. It's too bad. You know, when you study Greek drama, the word *hubris* comes up. It means false pride. I think that's what happened. I think they felt they could do no wrong and when you get into that situation, it usually ends up that you're wrong."

Shortly after the cancelation was announced, story editor Craig Van Sickle dreamily proposed future perceptions of the late series. "Who knows," he mused, "maybe we'll just have to be satisfied becoming like *The Prisoner* [1968–69]. Twenty years from now, it'll be a cult show with only those twenty-two episodes."

Not exactly, thankfully!

5 REBIRTH

The cancelation of *Alien Nation* was a mistake, and everybody knew it, from, expectedly, the show's cast and crew to, more surprisingly, many executives at Fox Broadcasting. Those who felt the same way also included the heads of the network's station affiliates who were extremely fond of *Alien Nation*. It was everyone's opinion that the series had the makings of another *Star Trek*, had it just been given the time to find an audience. The only person unconvinced was the guy who had canceled it in the first place, former Fox president Barry Diller. He didn't like the show, he didn't understand its appeal, and he saw no point in having it on his network.

As noted earlier, during the summer of 1990 pretty much everyone involved with *Alien Nation* was in a state of shock, not yet believing that they weren't going back to work on the series. Then Ken Johnson received an intriguing phone call. Supporters at the network, while refusing to admit that they had made a bad decision and still apparently trying to convince network head Barry Diller that theirs was the way to go, told Ken that they were interested in having a pair of two-hour TV movie scripts written which would allow *Alien Nation* to have all the creative scope that it needed. With Johnson supervising, Andrew Schneider and Diane Frolov started writing two made-for-TV movies: *Dark Horizon*, which would wrap up the TV series' cliffhanger, and *Body & Soul*, an attempt to explore the relationship between Sikes and Cathy.

"When they got the scripts, Fox really liked them," says Johnson. "Andy and Diane wrote some interesting stuff, a couple of startling new characters, and I think provided the opportunity to continue in the vein we were going and at the same time break a little new ground. It looked real promising at the time and everyone was saying *Dark Horizon* would go into production before Christmas 1990 or after the first of January 1991.

"The only thing Fox wanted in these scripts was something that would make it somewhat different than the [weekly] episodes," he adds. "Something that made it a little more of an event kind of quality. Sort of like saying, 'Okay, if it was a series, what was the stuff you would have done in the sweeps weeks?' And then to kind of fashion those into the two-hour scripts so that they would have a little more that they could promote, so that it doesn't just look like a two-hour-long episode. Those were the main things they were looking for."

At the time, Johnson discussed with this author the concepts behind both teleplays. *Dark Horizon* was a sequel of sorts to the episode "Contact" (TVS 08), in which an Overseer sends a signal into space to be received by a Tenctonese mothership. This film is the response to that signal.

"A new Newcomer arrives," explained Johnson in 1990. "The question becomes, from where and why? He becomes a formidable opponent to our people and, as a matter of fact, ends up moving into the Francisco household. They are unaware that he is who he is. He's a scout who has been sent to Earth because the message [from 'Contact'] was only partly received. He has come to sort of check out what the story is and if, indeed, there are people here that are worth taking. He is scoping out the situation and beginning to organize the enslavement of not only the Newcomers but the rest of humanity as well. It's *bad* news.

"His name is Ahpossno—a Russian word, actually, that means danger—and he's an interesting guy, sort of a cross between Albert Schweitzer and Bruce Lee, and he's a very compelling and sexy guy that Cathy begins to get a crush on. He's a soldier, a guy on a mission who has three dimensions to him. He's not unmoved by seeing George and Susan and their family, and how well they've adapted to Earth and how comfortable they are here. I think he has a couple of moments of soul-searching as to whether or not he's doing the right thing. Ultimately, though, he's a soldier and he has to do what he has to do. Our people finally realize who he is and what he's doing here, and they have got to stop him before he can take off and alert the others. It's interesting, because it builds on everything that we've done before."

Body & Soul, he explained, had a working title of "Sex With the Proper Alien."

"It's about sex and interbreeding, and it finally has Cathy and Sikes to the point where they want to try to have a relationship," Johnson detailed. "They sort of rush into it, even though Cathy has said that it could be dangerous for them to do so. Sikes says, 'Nah, I'm a jock. I can handle it.' The lights go out and we hear him scream. Next day, he walks into the police station with his neck bent at an odd angle and a very peculiar bruise. All the Newcomers immediately recognize it and say, 'Ah, you tried to ride a Tenctonese woman.' He's in trouble. The only way they can attempt to have sex is to go to a sex class that explains the differences in physiology and how to get it on with each other. It's very funny stuff.

"At the same time," he elaborated, "the episode opens very startlingly because there is a Newcomer giant, unlike any Newcomer we've seen before. He's over seven feet tall and is trying to escape from someone, and he's carrying an infant with him. He and the infant are separated and he disappears into the night after having killed somebody to protect the baby. The baby is very strange. It's not Newcomer but it's not human either. It seems in between. It may possibly be the first inter-species child, and this begins to cause quite a ruckus, which gets the Purists all uptight—as they tend to get—and raises the whole question of how interbreeding will ultimately affect our two races. It's sort of a compelling mystery as to who the baby is and how it came to be, what the relationship between the baby and the giant is—all of which comes to a startling conclusion."

All things seemed ready to move ahead, but once again the network intervened and pulled the plug at the last possible second. It's something that Johnson admits he had had a premonition of while swimming in his pool.

"It just occurred to me," he explains, "that everybody said yes to the scripts except for the guy [Barry Diller] who said no the last time. I had a sinking feeling and said, 'I bet he sandbags us again.' I felt that way because it was right at the very end and everybody had said yes. The interesting thing is that, to my knowledge, he never even read the scripts. Pretty amazing, isn't it? What I heard is that he just didn't feel that the show was going to do any better than it did the last time, which, incidentally, was better than several of his subsequent shows had been doing. Plus he didn't want to spend the money. The amazing thing is that they spent four months just having us develop the scripts. Why bother? He could have said the same thing four months earlier. I was under the impression that several people had asked him and that it was all fine. Then it occurred to me, 'Wait a minute, I haven't heard anything from Barry on this.' And there you go."

In the end, ironically, the fact that those two scripts were sitting in the Fox vaults gathering dust probably was the primary reason that *Alien Nation* returned to the air at all.

The eventual rebirth of *Alien Nation* began in early July 1993, when Lucy Salhaney, then chairperson of Fox Broadcasting, received a letter from Dorothy Swanson, the head of Viewers for Quality Television. Swanson commented that she had been watching Fox's *Lifepod* (1993), a sci-fi version of Alfred Hitchcock's *Lifeboat* (1944), and wondered why she wasn't watching an *Alien Nation* TV movie instead. She continued that VQT had not forgotten the late series and awaited its return with great anticipation. While that letter was not sufficient in itself to get the movies made, it certainly played a role in priming the pump at the network.

Salhaney, a longtime science-fiction fan, didn't require much encouragement. Interestingly, around the same time Fox had created an in-house production unit, Foxstar Productions, to fill the network's Tuesday Night Movie timeslot, and executives were sifting through the studio's tape library to see what would be appropriate source material. According to Foxstar executive Kevin Burns, Salhaney had chosen Steve Bell as the head of Foxstar, and Bell's list of dream projects was topped with *Alien Nation*.

"Steve got the go-ahead and called Ken Johnson," says Burns, "starting with the guy who executive-produced and directed the pilot for the series. As Steve remembers, he was concerned because after a year of working with Steven Bochco, trying to get Bochco's attention focused on *L.A. Law* [1986–94], he was afraid that Ken was going to say, 'I did that, been there, who cares? Good luck with it, Steve.' Steve was really impressed that Ken's attitude was, 'Thank God, I can't wait. When do we start?'"

Johnson recalls, "Steve Bell read the existing scripts, liked them, and asked us if we could make the first one a little bit bigger, so it would have even more of an event-like quality to it. I said, 'Sure, guys, open the cash register,' and they did—to my amazement. We got a healthy budget, about $4 million. It's funny, all of us doing the show did it under our quotes because we cared so much about getting it off the ground. The larger budget didn't go into any of our pockets, but it went into production value."

As Burns explains, he and Bell viewed every episode of the series, particularly the pilot, which they felt was better than the original 1988 feature film. They also looked at the cliffhanger episode ("Green Eyes," TVS 22), which presented, they felt, a formidable problem: how do you create a two-hour movie that not only satisfies the fans who have been waiting four years for a resolution to a cliffhanger, but also reaches a bigger audience than the one that the TV series had abandoned? To make the film successful, and because Fox now had a larger viewer base than it did in 1990, the studio needed to not only "preach" to the converted, but to reach new audiences while not annoying the old one.

"We had all these internal conversations," explains Burns. "'Can FBC run the cliffhanger the night before? How do we bring this in as a movie?' I wanted a movie, Steve wanted a movie that if somebody watched it for the first time, they'd get it and like it. The other thing, believe it or not, is that Steve did not have to go back to Ken Johnson. He could have taken *Alien Nation* and gone with some young kid director and a new writer that could have scrapped everything that had come before. Again, it's to Ken's credit and what he accomplished in terms of the series that we didn't consider that. I'm sensitive enough to see the fans satisfied. You don't leave people hanging for three or four years. We turned to *Dark Horizon*, which had been prepared as a Fox movie two or three years earlier for a very tight budget."

Upon reading the script, two things were apparent to Bell and Burns. First, the resolution of various cliffhangers from the show made sense when the script was originally written, but this was no longer so, since the familiarity on the audience's part wasn't the same as several years later. Second, the script just felt too small and confined.

"During the very first meeting with Ken, we said, 'Look, we want a movie, we want an event, yet it has to satisfy the fans and resolve the cliffhanger, yet it has to preach to the non-initiated.' A key to this, oddly enough, was the novelization of the *Dark Horizon* teleplay. We were kind of upset it existed, because there it was out there giving away the entire plot. The novel, I thought, used Andy and Diane's script, but it was the key to their script in that it took the cliffhanger episode and folded it into *Dark Horizon*. It combined the two and added scenes that a restricted budget could not have afforded. The author added scenes in deep space and other scenes taking place on the mothership. We read this novel and said, 'This is what the series, we thought, had been missing. The viewer or fan wants to see where the Tenctonese came from, what the Newcomers on Earth are afraid of, and what they're threatened to be brought back to.'

"Ken looked at us wearily," Burns adds, "because he's looking at two guys who are new in a way—who hadn't done a TV movie—and he had been burned so many times in the past. He'd had meeting after meeting and promises of *Alien Nation*. He's looking at Steve and me like, 'Are you guys two more idiots who are going to promise us you're going to get it on the air and we're going to get cheated again?' We told him what we wanted to see. We want to see Ahpossno getting his mission. We want to see the kind of things that the novel had. Ken said, and we respect his vision, 'This was never about technology. It was never about spaceships or hardware.' I said, 'You're absolutely right, but a lot has happened since *Alien Nation* went off the air. Look at *seaQuest, Deep*

Space Nine, and *Babylon 5* [1994–]. Audiences have become more sophisticated in a sense, they expect more from this genre on television, it's more affordable, oddly enough, because of the digital technology.'

"In other words, we were not coming in as Philistines trying to pollute the integrity of this project. On the other hand, we're coming in as producers and marketing people who say, 'We want footage for the promo. We want to show the audience something that the series couldn't do.' *Dark Horizon* is the *Alien Nation* they couldn't do before."

TV MOVIE EPISODE GUIDE

All the telefeatures are 120 minutes in length
Originally aired on Fox Broadcasting
Based on characters created by Rockne S. O'Bannon

TVM 01. "DARK HORIZON"

Original Airdate: October 25, 1994

PRODUCTION CREW

Executive Producer: Kenneth Johnson
Co-Producers: Diane Frolov and Andrew Schneider
Screenplay: Diane Frolov and Andrew Schneider
Director: Kenneth Johnson
Director of Photography: Lloyd Ahern II
Production Designer: Brenton Swift
Line Producer: Ron Mitchell
Editors: Alan Marks and David Strohmaier

Music:	David Kurtz
Sound:	Joe Kenworthy
Makeup:	Rick Stratton
Special Visual Effects:	Bob Millar

MAIN CAST

Gary Graham	(Matt Sikes)
Eric Pierpoint	(George Francisco)
Michele Scarabelli	(Susan Francisco)
Terri Treas	(Cathy Frankel)
Sean Six	(Buck Francisco)
Lauren Woodland	(Emily Francisco)
Jeff Marcus	(Albert Einstein)
Ron Fassler	(Captain Grazer)
Jenny Gago	(Beatrice Zapeda)

ADDITIONAL CAST

Susanna Thompson	(Lorraine Clark)
Michelle Lamar Richards	(Dr. Lois Allen)
Lee Bryant	(Phyllis Bryant)
Dana Anderson	(May O'Naise)
Scott Patterson	(Ahpossno)
Nina Foch	(Commander Burak)
Susan Appling	(Celinite Priestess)
Diane Civita	(Diane)

A Tenctonese soldier named Ahpossno comes to Earth to investigate the status of the aliens' lost slaves, following the receipt of a satellite transmission from the planet (sent during the series episode "Contact," TVS 08). It is his mission to see if the "merchandise" is still alive and, if so, to arrange for their retrieval, while arranging for the inhabitants of Earth to be taken as well.

At the same time, a Purist on a personal vendetta against George uses a virus to sicken—and nearly kill—Susan and Emily. It is the same virus that the Purists plan on making airborne in an attempt to wipe out the entire Tenctonese population. The two plots merge when Ahpossno arrives, helping Cathy in her attempts to stop the virus and, once the Purist problem is solved, driving a wedge between George and Susan as well as Sikes and Cathy. In the end, everything becomes a battle for the fate of *all* the inhabitants of Earth.

Commentary

Overall, *The Hollywood Reporter* enjoyed this first *Alien Nation* TV movie, noting, "Like all science fiction [it] says more about the present than any possible future. In spite of its rather heavy-handed, didactic approach to social issues, this is a fascinating two-hour telefilm that delivers its full entertainment value." Added *Variety*, "First hour takes care of the virus plot... and dismisses the Purist leader rather anticlimactically. Second hour shifts into a fight against the Tenctonese emissary, which is far more interesting, not to mention witty. This, too, is where the theme of prejudice against foreigners takes its most involving form, with focus switching from the futuristic equivalents of skinheads to Francisco's neighbors...."

AUTHOR'S RATING: ***½
Two scripts are obviously meshed together, and for the most part it works, as *Alien Nation* returns to the airwaves after a four-year absence. Writer-director Ken Johnson wisely discards Buck's affair with his history teacher and the whole Detective-Two rivalry from the episode "Green Eyes" (TVS

22), effectively restaging that segment's climax and retaining only the Purist threat of a virus that can be used against the Newcomers. Diane Frolov and Andrew Schneider's script successfully deals with that whole issue, while simultaneously picking up threads from "Contact" (TVS 08) by having a response to the partially-sent radio signal.

Ahpossno, in the form of actor Scott Patterson, is a terrific Tenctonese scout who has been sent to this Earth. His plan, to hand over not only the former slaves but also all of humanity to his superiors, is a truly frightening proposition, helped by Eric Pierpoint's effectively-staged realization that Ahpossno's people are en route to Earth for their cargo.

Amidst the action sequences in this telefeature are plenty of emotional moments as well: Sikes trying to reconcile with Cathy, while dealing with his feelings of jealousy toward Ahpossno; Buck bypassing his father and looking to the new arrival as the perfect Tenctonese role model; and Ahpossno's convincing Susan that her embracing of human culture is costing her own cultural identity.

One of the more disturbing aspects of this two-hour entry is the presentation of the Purists. These zealots are willing to sacrifice nearly a million innocent beings in their mission of "cleansing" the planet—all in the name of God. Most unsettling is the fact that this attitude is *not* far removed from the reality of our planet's recent history.

A major highlight of this film is finally giving the viewers the opportunity to get a more elaborate view of the Tenctonese spacecraft. Then, too, the actors, most notably Eric Pierpoint and Gary Graham, come back together on screen without missing a beat—the rapport is still there. Johnson deserves a lot of credit for reuniting the rest of the cast, a testament to the affection that the actors and the production crew maintained for *Alien Nation*.

Behind-the-Scenes

Dark Horizon actually began as a one-hour script written for the proposed second season of *Alien Nation.* Entitled "Soul Train," and written by Andrew Schneider and Diane Frolov, the story focused primarily on the Purist effort to wipe out the Newcomers, as well as the resolving of the various cliffhangers.

One of the most profound differences between the story's original incarnation and the final version seen on TV is the fact that many of the Tenctonese are beginning to walk around in a daze, losing their will to live. Cathy tells an inquiring Sikes that it's a syndrome known as Papayela, which is essentially a collective sense of doom. Her people sense that something dreadful is about to happen to them. Later, in a conversation with another police officer, Sikes confides, "Remember when they made George my partner? I wanted to move to Alaska. I'm still not used to them. I mean, let's face it—they're weird. But to think of life without them? I can't."

Buck's affair with his human teacher is pretty much dismissed in the story line, with the school's principal assigning her elsewhere, much to Buck's fury. The conflict between Sikes and George over the Detective-Two promotion and seniority issue is resolved when the duo realize that rank doesn't mean anything in comparison to almost losing Emily and Susan.

The next step in the script's evolution came in the aforementioned version written by Schneider and Frolov in 1990. While *very* close to the finished product, there are some significant differences as well. Most notably, the script does *not* open in deep space, instead allowing Ahpossno to basically already be on Earth. There is another scene in the film in which Ahpossno attempts to organize the Overseers. As originally written, during their meeting a delivery man arrives with two bags of food. Wanting to know if the gas used on the slaves to control their minds (discussed in "The Takeover," TVS 05) will work on humans, Ahpossno experiments on the unsuspecting man, ordering him to drive as quickly as he can into a brick wall. The man does as he's ordered, killing himself, and satisfying Ahpossno's curiosity.

There was also more in the telefeature to the sequences in which Ahpossno has basically convinced Susan that she needs to become one with her Tenctonese past and remove the human influences from her life. In the film, George throws Ahpossno out of the house when he realizes that the man is tearing apart his family. However, as originally conceived, Susan announces that she's leaving this house and, as is her right as the female of the household, is taking the children with her to a Tenctonese-only community in the mountains. George refuses to join them, as it goes against everything he believes in. The next day, Susan realizes the error she's about to make, when the Francisco station wagon arrives at the gates of New City. There are barbed-wire fences there, supposedly designed to keep humans out. Susan changes her mind about this living arrangement when the guard tells her that there are no human magazines or newspapers allowed inside, and the vehicle's cellular phone will have to be confiscated as well. Thus, there will be absolutely no contact with the human world. Knowing she can't live like this, she turns the car around and heads back home.

For the cast and crew of *Dark Horizon*, the joy of coming back to *Alien Nation* was tangible.

"We did a makeup test at the beginning of production," says executive producer-director Ken Johnson, "and our assistant director, who is a very smart, cool-headed woman not given to a lot of emotion, walked into the trailer, took one look at Eric in his George makeup, and burst into tears. She had not realized how much she'd missed George

Francisco, and we all felt the same way."

Eric Pierpoint concurs, "We looked around and couldn't believe it had been four years. It was like we were coming back from summer hiatus or something. Everybody's still got a good feeling about the project, about Ken, their characters, where they want to go. There's just a love for the show that is shared by every cast member."

Gary Graham remembers that the idea of a revival was first brought up to him the previous fall. "For many months I didn't want to get my hopes up," he admits. "I loved working with Kenny Johnson and Eric and the whole group, but we've been disappointed before and it was kind of like, 'Well, if it happens, it happens.' Finally, when we all showed up and were working and the aliens were in their heads, it was, 'Wow, Christmas came. Great.' And I've got to tell you, it's amazing. It's like we quit working a month ago. I guess they were characters that we loved so much that we never let them go."

What was challenging for both Pierpoint and Graham was the idea of stepping back into their respective characters, attempting to tap into their past while touching on the changes in their personal lives which would inevitably impact on their performances.

"I think that after you get off the pace of doing it every week or every day, and you have 'movie time' to make it, then you sort of start over," offers Pierpoint. "I think it's necessary to strip it back down and make sure that wherever the character is coming from, it's coming honestly and isn't a comment on what worked before. That it isn't your body remembering what worked and going into that mode automatically. At the time, I didn't know what the next evolution would be. I tried not to make too many decisions ahead of time, because one of the best things that happens in this show is we start creating spontaneously. Gary and I are almost like a vaudeville team in the sense that it's a partnership where we play into each other's strengths. He's a terrific straight man. I always said to him that Matt and George and Eric and Gary made each other better."

For his part, Graham notes, "The major thing that happened to me is that I became a daddy. I got married and we had a little girl, and that just changes your whole perspective as a human being. I can't imagine it not also affecting my portrayal of Sikes. He might not be the old curmudgeon that we remember. He's still the guy who eternally wakes up on the wrong side of the bed, but there's a new depth of compassion, perhaps, in his psyche. In a sense, he's come out of the closet in this movie, because he is very much a friend of Newcomers."

Like Pierpoint, Graham believes that there is indeed a creative spark between them and that it comes across on film. "Eric is a very giving performer," he says, "always inventive, always looking to discover in the scene. He's kind of a high-wire walker like I am, where we like to discover when the cameras are rolling.... As far as the acting goes, you know who your character is only when the camera is rolling. That's who you are and that's what's captured forever. Eric would give and take and listen. We just loved the Matt and George stuff, just our relationship. The gist of the show, as far as we were both concerned, has always been the relationship between Matt and George."

Which probably didn't make things easy for the newcomer to the *Alien Nation* family, former baseball-player-turned-actor Scott Patterson, essaying the role of Ahpossno.

"I knew I was coming into a family situation," says Patterson. "They had all done the series and were happy to see each other, while I was a newcomer, as well I should be, considering the role. Everyone was really supportive. I had a lot of questions about the Tenctonese language, about their customs and their rituals, and they were more than helpful. I was overwhelmed by their support."

He admits to having been extremely enthusiastic about his role as Ahpossno and his involvement in the project.

"The part was a challenge," he reflects, "and it was a chance to flex my acting muscles, because you're in that makeup so much of the time. Eric Pierpoint gave me some advice about the makeup. He said, 'Let the makeup do a lot of it. There's not much you have to do if you accept the fact that the script is well-written, you trust your director, and you're surrounded by good actors.' I also thought that the character's arc was terrific, as he was becoming aware of some kind of emotional life that had been buried for years and years. There's just terrific conflict in him. He's always fighting against some buried self, some unknown self."

One common theme among reviewers that intrigued Patterson was the press's constant reference to Ahpossno being the film's bad guy.

"He's *not* a bad guy," the actor emphasizes. "I never saw him as the villain. I saw him as somebody simply doing a job. It's not a pleasant job, but it's a necessary one. And that's how he sees it. Let's say you get a chance to play Adolph Hitler. If you play him as an evil man, you're going to fail miserably. *He* thought he was *saving* Germany. So that's how it has to be played, otherwise you can't find the man. You can't make him human or find any vulnerability or humor. This is what Kenny and I tried to do."

An aspect of *Dark Horizon* that Pierpoint enjoyed was what he felt was the evolution of the human *and* Tenctonese points of view.

"I think Sikes is more relaxed than he was," says Pierpoint. "He's suspicious of what's going on, not because Ahpossno is a Newcomer, but because of who he is as a person. Certain things are bound to happen. One is that Sikes and other humans will become more relaxed about the alien environment, and the opposite to that is the aliens start to shed more of their traditions and become almost more human. What I was trying to do was provide that link between the Ahpossno character and humans. I think probably by now George is becoming more and more humanized. We did a couple of spontaneous moments and picked up a couple of shots that I think are pretty indicative of how entrenched in the world he is and how adaptive he has become.

"There's one scene where we're all kind of arriving at the Francisco home after the hospital. I looked at this house and walked up to Kenny and said, 'You know, we can pick up a really interesting shot here. George is so proud of this disgustingly middle-class house, that before he goes in he takes a breath, looks at Ahpossno, and says, 'It's nice, isn't it?', and Ahpossno just has this strange expression on his face. So he's very proud of his accomplishments. That's the direction George is heading, domestically."

TVM 02. "Body & Soul"

Original Airdate: October 10, 1995

PRODUCTION CREW

Executive Producer:	Kenneth Johnson
Producer:	Paul Kurta
Supervising Producer:	Bob Lemchen
Screenplay:	Renee and Harry Longstreet, Diane Frolov, and Andrew Schneider
Director:	Kenneth Johnson
Director of Photography:	Shelly Johnson

Production Designer:	Colin D. Irwin
Editor:	Ian C. Marks
Music:	David Kurtz

MAIN CAST

Gary Graham	(Matt Sikes)
Eric Pierpoint	(George Francisco)
Michele Scarabelli	(Susan Francisco)
Terri Treas	(Cathy Frankel)
Sean Six	(Buck Francisco)
Lauren Woodland	(Emily Francisco)
Jeff Marcus	(Albert Einstein)
Ron Fassler	(Captain Grazer)
Jenny Gago	(Beatrice Zapeda)

ADDITIONAL CAST

Josie Kim	(Dr. Lois Allen)
Tiny Ron	(The Giant)
Aimee and Danielle Warren	(The Child)
Pamela Gordon	(Dr. Adrian Tivoli)
Leon Russom	(Benson)
Kristin Davis	(Karina Tivoli)

Sikes decides that he wants more than a platonic relationship with Cathy, but finds the classes he'll need to take if he's going to survive sex with a Newcomer are a little daunting. Meanwhile, two Newcomers—a giant and a child—escape from a top-secret complex. When the child is taken into custody, Purists fear that a Tenctonese-human hybrid has been achieved, while the name Cherboke causes an outbreak of fear in the Newcomer community.

Sikes and George are assigned to the case, which seems to involve famed Newcomer scientist Dr. Tivoli. George fears for his family's safety as the investigation continues, but he ultimately realizes he cannot conceal the truth of what he learns: the U.S. is using Tenctonese technology to create an ultimate weapon, a laser device.

NOTE: An earlier draft of *Body & Soul* had Sikes having a surreal dream in which he and Cathy are having a romantic dinner on the roof of their building. They break into a romantic dance and, in the midst of it, Cathy suddenly becomes human and Sikes becomes a Tenctonese!

Commentary

The Hollywood Reporter enjoyed the second *Alien Nation* film, noting that *Body & Soul* is "...well-produced and philosophically absorbing. Like all good science fiction, the plot is a convenient cover for the exploration of current social concerns. The film is an extended consideration of how to reconcile differences, both within and between individuals.... The script treats issues of diversity and unity between beings in a somewhat less sophisticated way. Arguments over interspecies unions mirror those over interracial relationships, but in a somewhat simplistic and unconvincing way. Otherwise, the dialogue is well-written and believable...." Added *TV Guide*, "The second movie sequel to the former sci-fi series improves upon the first.... The script is clever and engaging, while Sikes and Francisco again prove to be a terrific comic tandem."

AUTHOR'S RATING: ***

It's difficult not feeling pride at watching our former racist, Matthew Sikes, finally take his first full-blown steps into maturity as he and Cathy take their relationship to the next level. A lot of humor is mined from their attending a sex-education class, particularly Graham's wonderful exasperation when he is hit with one humiliating question after another, such as "How long is your penis when fully erect?" His look of desperation as he tries to get out of the classroom is hysterical.

Another theme successfully raised in the episode is the controversy surrounding possible inter-species procreation, with members of both the Tenctonese and human communities protesting such mating as signaling the end of their respective species.

The part of the story line devoted to Cherboke's experiments, most notably the Newcomer giant and infant, is a bit convoluted and, at times, just plain confusing. Nonetheless, it works, as it hints at the atrocities the slaves once underwent while working for the Overseers. What falls absolutely flat, however, in the plot line is the "big gun" Tenctonese laser. It's obvious that Fox pumped extra production dollars into the budget and they wanted another world-threatening plot point. Still, this story line is so blatantly tacked onto the episode plot that it emerges as nothing more than a distraction. Once again, in retrospect, character developments and interactions are what save the day for this second feature.

Behind-the-Scenes

In discussing how *Body & Soul* developed from its original conception as a 1990 TV-movie script to one that aired five years later, director Ken Johnson points out, "Both versions focus on a Mengele-sort-of-character who had been performing experiments on the ship, and continued once he got to Earth. They also involve a hybrid baby and a giant, which were actually two parts of the same creature. What we tried to do in the final version was expand the premise of that to deal with geniuses in society. But does their genius make them immune from prosecution once the war is over? It explores the people who worked for and with, and were Overseers in, the slave world, but whose genius in their various expertises, if there is such a word, made them valuable commodities to the victors of war. Or, in this case, the government and private enterprise here on the planet where they have washed ashore. It sort of investigates what is appropriate. Can one take advantage of resourceful people or are they indeed war criminals? It's an intriguing notion that we're going to expand on a bit more. In the course of that, we will discover that there are large portions of the slave ship still existing that the government has hidden away or is in the hands of private enterprise.

"While that may be the groundwork for something in the future," he adds, "it gives us a chance to capitalize on the alien imagery that our show can do rather organically and naturally without anybody looking too far for it, like *The X-Files* has to. The advantage we have over *The X-Files* is that our aliens are right there in your face. That's the plan and direction. At the same time, we're exploring the whole reaction that both humans and the Newcomers have regarding the first inter-species baby and how that affects the sexuality that Sikes and Cathy are going through."

One of the original script writers, Diane Frolov, explains: "Our original draft of the script was a little more intimate. It didn't have the whole weapon thing and stuff being blown up. It was really exploring the whole idea of what is the body and what is the soul, and creating a creature that was severed. I think the laser-gun idea was designed to raise the stakes again, that the world was going to be imperiled. We didn't have that originally."

"What we liked about the idea," adds the other original scripter, Andrew Schneider, "was that there was a creature that appeared to be two creatures but was, in fact, one. That was a very intriguing notion to us, and that's primarily what it was about. What is the nature of existence of your personality and identity? But the network wanted some bigger issues."

Eric Pierpoint notes, "*Body & Soul* had some really heavy subject matter in terms of this Mengele-like character; a doctor experimenting in ways of distorting the Tenctonese mind and body, basically seeing what he could mutate just for fun with these hellacious experiments. It was an interesting script, though speaking with the network it seems they really do put pressure on us to develop larger-than-life story lines, in the sense that there has to be a big, overall event. They feel they can't sustain it with just the characters."

As mentioned earlier, the two characters who are really showcased are Sikes and Cathy, which sparks Gary Graham's wish list for the future. "*Body & Soul* opened up a lot of things," he says. "Cathy and Matt are finally getting together. Maybe there are wedding bells in the air. Matt Sikes has a Catholic background. Sooner or later it's going to play on his conscience. I'm married, it played on mine. He can't go to these levels of intimacy without making a final commitment. Down the line, who knows? Maybe there will be an interspecies newborn. The episode deals with my concerns and weirdness about it, and confronting that will be interesting."

Surprisingly, director Ken Johnson had a moment's hesitation about signing up for the back-to-back shooting of *Body & Soul* and the next made-for-TV film, *Millennium*.

"After doing the pilot," he explains, "then the series, and then *Dark Horizon*, part of me thought, 'Gee, I've sort of done this before. Can I get my enthusiasm up again?' But it came so easily because the cast are all people that I adore, who love each other. There are no jerks. Everybody cares about each other, the crew is terrific, and these two stories are splendid and get us into territories that we haven't gotten into before. So it's a continuation of all that's wonderful about *Alien Nation*, plus breaking some new ground at the same time.

"Bringing the cast back together is one of the most glorious experiences of the whole process," he adds. "They care about each other, they're supportive of each other, and know their characters even better than we do who write them. When they got together this time in my dining room to read the script, it was like no time had passed. It's kind of frustrating for me, because I sit there and say, 'What do I have to do to direct?' There's no directing to do. They're already there."

TVM 03. "MILLENNIUM"

Original Airdate: January 2, 1996

PRODUCTION CREW

Executive Producer: Kenneth Johnson
Producer: Paul Kurta
Screenplay: Kenneth Johnson
Director: Kenneth Johnson
Director of Photography: Shelly Johnson
Production Designer: Colin D. Irwin
Editor: David Strohmaier
Music: David Kurtz
Stunt Coordinator: Jon Epstein

MAIN CAST

Gary Graham (Matt Sikes)
Eric Pierpoint (George Francisco)
Michele Scarabelli (Susan Francisco)
Terri Treas (Cathy Frankel)
Sean Six (Buck Francisco)

Lauren Woodland	(Emily Francisco)
Jeff Marcus	(Albert Einstein)
Ron Fassler	(Captain Grazer)
Jenny Gago	(Beatrice Zapeda)

ADDITIONAL CAST

Risa Shiffman	(Jill)
Kerrie Keane	(Jennifer)
Steve Flynn	(Calaban)
Herta Ware	(Alana)
David Faustino	(Felix)
Susan Graham Lavelle	(Polly Wannakraker)
Rick Snyder	(Bigelow)

It's the final week of the twentieth century and society feels like it is falling apart. A Tenctonese artifact known as the Portal (a small box with great mystical powers), intended as a religious teaching aid, has fallen into the hands of an underground cult and is being used to lure victims into the ultimate trip. Its spiritual promise, however, hides a far deadlier secret that could cost numerous people—including Buck Francisco—their lives, unless George and Sikes can stop the cult leader who is manipulating innocents for profit.

Commentary

TV Guide enthused over *Millennium*: "Basically a crime story about a devious sect, this... TV-movie sequel to the sci-fi series is also an intriguing study in interplanetary assimilation." *The New York Times*' John J. O'Connor added, "... Welcome to *Alien Nation*, a clever and often witty sci-fi look at Newcomers: visitors to Earth who are nutritionally dependent on sour milk and are remarkably virtuous and industrious but just different enough to make ordinary citizens edgy. Welcome to American xenophobia in the 1990's. . . ." Finally, *The Hollywood Reporter* noted, "More than any other science-fiction program, *Alien Nation* is the inheritor of the *Star Trek* mantle—though not because of its visual style, characterizations or plot structure. Rather, the similarity rests on the way the show's stories use the future to explore pressing issues of the present. . . . Director Kenneth Johnson does a great job on the visual look of *Millennium*, but the performances are problematic—overamped, overdramatic and choppy. Johnson did a fine job helping the actors play their roles in exotic settings so that they convey a believable sense of wonder and terror. . . ."

AUTHOR'S RATING: ****
The best of the *Alien Nation* TV movies, *Millennium* does what the series always did best: intertwining a hard-hitting allegory about society with this show's own unique characterizations.

To begin with, there's something satisfying about Ken Johnson and company returning to the series and providing continuity for the films by utilizing plot lines of this saga begun in the weekly TV series. In this case, it's the Portal initially presented in the episode "Generation to Generation" (TVS 14). Designed as a religious object, it makes perfect sense for a Tenctonese to try to use it for personal gain (once again, our influence on the aliens), regardless of the deaths she will create among innocent people. Sean Six gives his best performance as Buck Francisco, the teenager who has spent much of the series as a lost soul and who is betrayed repeatedly by life and those around him.

"*Millennium* is no exception. Here, Buck feels that he has found religious enlightenment and a strong connection to his heritage. Yet, once again, his emotions and ongoing need for self-identity are completely exploited. Lauren Woodland's

Emily also shines in this TV movie as she begins dating a human teen. She, in turn, is ultimately devastated when she learns that he's only interested in her because he wants to "bag a Slag." Her dramatic reaction to this discovery is heartbreaking.

The interplay between costars Gary Graham and Eric Pierpoint is back where it should be, the creative spark between them as bright as ever. In addition, there are many humorous moments in this entry, such as when George maxes out his credit cards and is at a loss as to what to do financially, and when Sikes attempts to write his Detective-Two required essay without doing any real work toward that goal. Ron Fassler's Captain Grazer in this installment also gets to do more than just say, "Francisco, Sikes, you've got a murder." In *Millennium* he attempts to take the Portal and use it to create a futuristic Disneyland, and is quite funny in his greed. Guest star Kerrie Keane is effectively cold-hearted as the Tenctonese woman/"Priestess" once rejected by society, who now takes great pleasure in what she is doing with the Portal.

Executive producer Ken Johnson, in particular, is especially charged up for this production, writing and directing one of his best series' efforts. Despite the fact that this story is heavy in special effects, he never loses sight of the human element of the plot. All in all, *Millennium* was a great job by everyone.

Behind-the-Scenes

Essentially a sequel to the episode "Generation to Generation" (TVS 14), *Millennium* deals with the power of a small Tenctonese device that serves as a portal to Tencton.

"This Newcomer religious device creates an incredible virtual reality," says director-writer Ken Johnson, "where someone can literally transport into various alien environments. It was designed to aid in spiritual enlightenment, but if the Portal is misused, it can become far more dangerous than LSD, and in the hands of a charismatic cult leader it becomes outright deadly. The story is set in the last week of the millennium, when the world is going nuts anyway. Some people think it's the end of the world, some people think the aliens are the new Christ coming to save us, and other people think they're Satan.

"What the story's about, really, is instant gratification," he continues. "Our theme here is society's growing need for instant gratification, and that resonates through the whole story and impacts on all of the characters. The Portal itself is designed to be used like a Zen Master would use something. You can't become a black belt overnight. The problem is that Buck and a lot of the other people that are sucked into this cult want enlightenment and they want it now. Emily wants a new synthesizer so she can play in a band, now! Matthew is finally taking his Detective-Two test again, and has to write this research report. He discovers that Cathy has this cool computer program called 'Term Writer,' in which you write a few things, enter your resources, and it writes your term paper.

"George has been caught up in technology. He's always got to have the newest computer. Susan is always on his case, saying, 'George, you've got to get away from this slave mentality,' which is like the Depression mentality we went through with our parents. My father until the end of his life would always steal crackers off the table. At the same time, Susan is working in advertising, which is all about—guess what?—instant gratification. I'm very proud of the story."

Characterization was prominent on Eric Pierpoint's mind during production. "This one really goes back to the character realm," offers the actor. "There's more relationship going on with the family, more stuff going on between Matt and

George, as well as more friction. There's a lot of opportunity for the character, and by-play that we really, really need and has not been the focus since the series. We need that, because the previous films were so event-driven. Kenny really fights for the character by-play, and I know the network realizes that's what it needs too. It's a tough balance. It's like the original movie with James Caan and Mandy Patinkin. The first part of the movie is character setup and the second half goes off in another direction, a cop movie. Therefore, you lose what's interesting, because everybody can make a cop movie. It's no big deal. But to do something about the characters is a bigger challenge.

"Some of it is kind of a love story between two men that's okay to look at. I think that's an interesting interpretation of it. I hadn't quite thought of it that way, but I guess that's what it is. They love the best of each other, and put up with the foibles and pressures of the other half. They're best friends, and more and more as men we think that's okay. It's more okay than it used to be, especially doing it this way which is protected because you can project all kinds of things onto an alien. You can make it safe; it's safe, in a sense, to do the character."

Gary Graham chuckles as he reflects on his feelings reading the *Millennium* script for the first time. "This is not to take anything away from Kenny," he says. "There's something that drives actors nuts. Kenny likes to vernacularize his dialogue as the character speaks. I'm reading these things and it's really hard to get through because it's 'way ta go', 'wanna', 'gotta', and all this vernacular speech. I say, 'Kenny, I can barely read this,' and he says, 'Well, that's the way you speak.' 'I know, but let me make the decision to speak that way.' We had a big old, good-natured fight about it right in front of the whole cast. I was actually being funny, but it sets my teeth on edge to read stuff like that.

"When you get past all that, the script ended up being very good and I didn't know it was very good until we were filming it and it all came together. I saw the intensity of the performances and the lighting setups and the locations and all that. About two-thirds through, I said, 'Oh, this is going to be a *good* movie.' In fact, I think it's the best of the first three, which surprised me because I thought *Body & Soul* was so good. *Millennium* was actually more exciting and it dealt with larger issues."

TVM 04. "THE ENEMY WITHIN"

Original Airdate: October 15, 1996

PRODUCTION CREW

Executive Producer:	Kenneth Johnson
Producer:	Ron Mitchell
Screenplay:	Diane Frolov and Andrew Schneider
Director:	Kenneth Johnson
Director of Photography:	Ron Garcia
Production Designer:	Colin D. Irwin
Editor:	David Strohmaier
Music:	Steve Dorff
Stunt Coordinator:	Jon Epstein

MAIN CAST

Gary Graham	(Matt Sikes)
Eric Pierpoint	(George Francisco)
Michele Scarabelli	(Susan Francisco)
Terri Treas	(Cathy Frankel)
Sean Six	(Buck Francisco)
Lauren Woodland	(Emily Francisco)

Jeff Marcus (Albert Einstein)
Ron Fassler (Captain Grazer)
Jenny Gago (Beatrice Zapeda)

ADDITIONAL CAST

Kerrie Keane (Jessica Partridge)
Tiny Ron (Queen Mother)
Joe Lando (Rick Shaw)
Wayne Pere (Terry Firma)
Dana Anderson (May O'Naise)
Bridgitta Dau (Carrie Onbag)
Darin Heames (Soren Kierkegaard)

Susan and George's marriage is tested when Albert and May ask George to act as the Binnaum for their child. At the same time, the death of a Newcomer girl is linked to a group of subterranean Tenctonese outcasts known as the Eenos. The Eenos are despised by all Newcomers, including the usually unprejudiced George, and accused of cannibalism while aboard the ship. Sikes and George (the latter reluctantly) investigate beneath the streets of Los Angeles, where they encounter a thriving Newcomer society made up of the Eenos and a mutated being known as the Queen Mother. She seems to have nothing less than world domination on her mind.

Commentary

While *TV Guide* rated *The Enemy Within* as "engaging," the *Hollywood Reporter* wasn't as kind, noting, "...The script...is too formulaic to be entirely enjoyable. The recurring topical serendipity and intensity of focus makes it difficult to entirely suspend disbelief. Polished performances by Gary Graham and [Eric Pierpoint] go a long way toward making the show work.... The real star of this show, however, is Kenneth Johnson's extraordinary work as a director.... The team delivers the most astonishing images ever produced on the show."

AUTHOR'S RATING: **½

Despite the array of special effects on *Alien Nation*, the most stunning aspect of *The Enemy Within* is, nonetheless, the revelation of George's prejudice against the Eenos. It is a difficult character trait for Eric Pierpoint to undertake, as George has never come across as anything but the most tolerant being in the universe, next to Gandhi and Mother Teresa. What's also nice is the actor's role-reversal, to some degree, with Gary Graham, as Sikes finds himself in the unusual position of having to defend the underdog.

For Sikes and Cathy there is continuing growth and change as they move in together and explore the challenges of this new arrangement. Cathy tries to make herself comfortable in Sikes's apartment, and soon takes control of the situation and his apartment. It is extremely touching, later, when Sikes thinks that she's having an affair. He confronts her at a hotel, only to learn that she has been renting a room so she can have her own space and not be in his way. His solution is a moving one, and goes a long way in continuing the evolution of this dimensional character.

Unfortunately, *The Enemy Within* has its share of plot problems as well. First, having *Body & Soul*'s Tiny Ron return to *Alien Nation*, this time playing the Queen Mother, is a *major* mistake. This is a character that begged to be created via computer rather than be played by a human, so that it would truly be something otherworldly. Instead, it looks like something out of *The Toxic Avenger* (1986), and, in turn, is distracting to the viewer. Of course, there were most likely budget considerations, but this still seems like a pivotal creative mistake.

This entry also integrates the Francisco family into the story to a greater degree than usual, to the point of stretching credibility. Emily befriends an Eeno whom George rejects, and an attack on the kids finally opens his eyes, while Buck is the one who leads them to the climactic encounter with the Queen Mother. Conversely, the sexual strains on the Francisco marriage are very credible and seem a natural and *honest* story development.

Behind-the-Scenes

"When we were doing the series," explains co-scripter Andrew Schneider, "Diane really wanted to do a story about cannibals. There was a group of Newcomer cannibals who were pariahs, but nobody wanted to do the story. The network thought it was too grim and too horrifying. Kenny was reluctant to do it, but it never left Diane's heart. She finally got the chance with this script to develop the Eenos. The other thing that made it work for us is George's prejudice. George has always been this paragon of goodwill, and to see that he has a racist side was good juice for the story because it was an unexpected side of his personality."

As director Ken Johnson explains it, the plot of this two-hour entry can really by summarized by its title. "It's about the fact that all of us have various enemies within ourselves," he says, "and if we don't confront them and deal with them, they can eat you up from the inside. Everybody's going through that in this story: Buck and his lack of focus and frustration at trying to figure out who he is; Susan is having some real negative image problems, and there seems to be a lack of interest from her husband, which sort of skews her to another Newcomer, Rick Shaw.... Cathy and Matt move in together and face the problems they have to deal with there. So everybody is dealing with issues from within."

Gary Graham enjoyed swapping character traits with Eric Pierpoint for this episode, allowing Sikes to be the tolerant one of the duo this time out. "The Eenos are shunned by the other Newcomers," he explains, "particularly by George. That's his monkey to wrestle with and I call him on it, I'm proud to say. Our show is a metaphor for interracial relationships, in this case inter-species relationships. Quite often those who trumpet the cause of integration, and racial and species tolerance, are themselves fraught with hypocrisy."

After some initial reluctance, Pierpoint himself embraced that element of the script. "*The Enemy Within* is interesting because what we have to do with these two-hour movies is put on a humongous, world-threatening event, which is tough. It stretches reality so much that it seems a little cartoony to me. I understand why they're doing it, because the people who are not *Alien Nation* fanatics, or people who don't normally watch it, want to watch something complete and entertaining. Kenny was saying this to the press: If we were doing a weekly series this wouldn't be part of it. But because we've got a bigger budget and have more time, we can. The network thinks we'll get more of an audience.

"When I read the script," he continues, "I thought, 'No, you can't do this to George. George would be beyond something like this.' But it's the *perfect* thing, because it's where you'd least expect it. You don't even know what difference he's seeing between the Eenos and the other Tenctonese. He's judging like anybody else would judge, emotionally, based on something that was happening to him and his people at a terrible time. You can't even tell the difference, but he can. Then to have him show that part of his personality, that he is unmoving, to have him not even willing to listen, is great because you've got values handed down from generation to generation. His kids don't believe what he believes, he just accepts it carte blanche. Thank God, they turn him around.

"But the wonderful thing about Matt and George, to me, is that relationship which comes into play here. Here you've got George, who was the one with all of these words in previous episodes during the series where he's talking about judging men and women and having stereotypical attitudes about them, but Matt having them anyway. George doesn't understand the racism inherent in humans. Now the tables are turned and Matt is sitting there telling him, and he's not willing to listen until he finally comes face to face with it. I like that about them. I think there are not as many discussions between Matt and George about philosophy as there have been in previous scripts because it seems like a lot of the dynamics are happening outside of that relationship. I think that's a mistake, but I guess you can't play the same part all the time. When we do get together, the banter is like a half-page scene and no longer three pages."

TVM 05. "THE UDARA LEGACY"

Original Airdate: July 29, 1997

PRODUCTION CREW

Executive Producer: Kenneth Johnson
Producer: Ron Mitchell
Screenplay: Renee and Harry Longstreet
Director: Kenneth Johnson
Director of Photography: Ron Garcia
Production Designer: Colin D. Irwin
Editor: Alan Marks
Music: Steve Dorff

Stunt Coordinator: Jon Epstein

MAIN CAST

Gary Graham (Matt Sikes)
Eric Pierpoint (George Francisco)
Michele Scarabelli (Susan Francisco)
Terri Treas (Cathy Frankel)
Sean Six (Buck Francisco)
Lauren Woodland (Emily Francisco)
Jeff Marcus (Albert Einstein)
Ron Fassler (Captain Grazer)
Jenny Gago (Beatrice Zapeda)

ADDITIONAL CAST

Lane Smith (Senator Silverthorne)
Peggy McCay (Avra)
Mary Ann Onedy (Tina)
Scotch Ellis Loring (Gary)
Mailon Rivera (Andrews)

On board the slave ship, an underground movement called the Udara fought a war of attrition against the Overseers. Some Udara were unknowingly programmed so they could be controlled to continue the fight, unaware of their subsequent actions. On Earth, the secret of this brainwashing has been found and has been reactivated. It is learned for the first time that Susan Francisco was a member of Udara, and she had had Emily seeded as a child prior to their landing on Earth. Now *someone* has figured out a way to activate these assassins, and Emily is one of their weapons.

Meanwhile, Buck finally discovers his purpose in life by joining the police academy and following in his father's professional footsteps.

Commentary

"This blending of sci-fi and cop-show formulas works because the pondering is thoughtful and softened by wit," said *TV Guide*. "The cop-show part holds up, too—until the last half hour, when the plot turns coincidental and melodramatic."

AUTHOR'S RATING: ***

Once again we're given a glimpse of what life was like on the slave ship for the Tenctonese, and *The Udara Legacy* shows us that it really wasn't such a great place to be (although that's something we've been well aware of all along). Despite similarities between this story line and those of *The Manchurian Candidate* (1962) and *Telefon* (1971), the need for an assassin squad in such a situation makes perfect sense. The fact that Susan Francisco is a member of Udara and has kept it a secret just adds depth to her character. At the same time, it opens up—at least temporarily—some genuine conflict between her and George that goes far beyond the "he's not paying enough attention to me" syndrome of the earlier *The Enemy Within* (TVM 04).

George's rage at learning this secret is nicely handled by Eric Pierpoint. As always, he manages to stay sympathetic no matter how emotional he gets. The real acting stand-out, though, is Michele Scarabelli, who offers her best performance on the series to date. It is wonderful watching her work up the courage to tell George the truth, providing her heartfelt explanation as to why she became Udara and tearfully rationalizing why she had had Emily seeded. There is also an electric confrontation in the precinct interrogation room between Susan and Avra, the head of the Udara. It is so well-handled that it seems, for at least a moment, that Susan will kill this woman right in front of everyone. Terrific stuff!

Buck's joining the police academy is an interesting plot irony, considering the resentment he felt toward his father during the early days of the series, when he accused him of selling-out his own race by joining with the humans. The only drawback to this story point is that it continues the plot contrivance of involving the rest of the Francisco family in these adventures, not the least of whom is Emily, having been seeded as Udara. Ultimately, she plays a pivotal role in the story as she attempts to assassinate Senator Silverthorne, but ends up shooting her brother, Buck, in the process.

Probably the biggest disappointment of this film is the lack of true story involvement for the Sikes character. Gary Graham has very little to do, and what he is given to perform—obsessing over a car that he's long dreamed of owning—is totally repetitious of what he did in the episode "Gimme, Gimme" (TVS 20). As important as the Francisco family is to this TV series, it is the Sikes-George relationship that is truly the heart and soul of *Alien Nation*. When that is not exploited, the effect is damaging to the film as a whole, as it was when it occurred in the TV-series episodes.

Behind-the-Scenes

While admitting that *The Udara Legacy* has certain thematic elements in common with the series episode "The Red Room" (TVS 12), Kenneth Johnson feels there are some fairly significant differences presented here as well.

"'The Red Room' was about contemporary American technology trying to take advantage of George and some others and turning them into killing machines," he says. "This is different and actually was originated for a good cause. It was originated by the Japanese Warrior among the slaves, fighting in a resistance movement to overcome the gas that has kept them docile. Once they landed here, all the Newcomers that had been seeded with this psychological gene sort of melted into society. Well, now somebody's gotten a hold of the list and is using it for nefarious purposes. The startling thing we discover, of course, is that it was a great honor to be chosen to be one of these subjects among the resistance. We find out that Susan had Emily seeded, so we've got Emily on a suicide mission to create the greatest race riot in the history of Los Angeles.

"It's really a film about control," he elaborates, "even to the point in the Matt and Cathy story where it's a fight over the remote control. That little theme resonates all the way through it. We also get into the issue of Susan being in Udara, so we begin asking the question: When do you draw the line? How far is too far when you're fighting back against the bad guy? When do you become a bad guy yourself in terms of fighting back? To my delight, both the studio and the network are beginning to notice that what really makes the show sing is when the Francisco family sits around the dinner table together, as well as the Matt and George material."

At this point, though, both Gary Graham and Eric Pierpoint have noticed that the Sikes-and-George dynamic is definitely taking a back seat to other characters and events in the films.

"As I've been known to say to Eric, 'Hey, we de *Alien Nation,*'" laughs Graham. "'Who is this Ahpossno guy? Who are all these other people? We de *Alien Nation.*'"

Adds Pierpoint, "The Matt-and-George relationship is the strength of *Alien Nation*. The other stuff is interesting, but it's B-story, really. It shouldn't be the A story. I think they know that, but they're trying something different. I was talking to Kenny about a script idea in which George is captured or held hostage by Purists and Matt and George are separated, with Matt trying to rescue him. Kenny said, 'We don't want to keep you guys apart.' I said, 'You're right. So stop keeping us apart.'

I recently watched *Body & Soul* and that had a lot of the Matt and Cathy sexual things. I thought that was a fun thing as a B story. What happens in *Udara Legacy* is you've got the family as the A story, which sets up a different rhythm. You've got George and his family rather than Matt and George. And the stuff they've done with Matt with his car in the episode is a little repetitive. Sometimes I say that everybody needs to watch all the episodes and look at what we've already done.

"*Udara* was a little tough for the George character," he adds. "He finds out that he is living with a rebel who has killed and his moral implant has to come to terms with the right and wrong of it. He does eventually come around and see that he was wrong to judge because of the circumstances, and he's helped to that discovery by Matt. I struggled with it because it's different. It makes George less the voice of reason and more the voice of irrationality, and Matt the voice of reason. Which I like on occasion. The problem is that it's hard to feed all the mouths and make everybody happy. Both Sean [Six] and Lauren [Woodland] are getting more and more action. There's also the problem, as I've said, of having them save the world every episode. You make it interesting by really good writing and making sure the proper dynamics are in place. If you try to go too big, then you don't get that by-play and banter.

"If you look at *Star Trek*, not to disrespect the spin-offs, and really look at Kirk and Spock, you realize you've got to have those guys together because it doesn't work unless they are. *Star Trek: The Next Generation* doesn't have that. They have to rely on the other stuff that *Star Trek* consists of. It's not rooted in the same relationship. I think the only reason to watch *Star Trek*, for me, is to watch William Shatner and Leonard Nimoy, because that was always the most fun. I really believe that they know this, but it's tough to hit a home run every time. You might hit a double off a wall and that's okay too, but I want a home run. I know it sounds like I'm bitching, but I'm not. I just think that rather than having the family go through trying to figure it out, I really think it should be Matt-and-George, together, trying to figure it out. There is evidence of that, but not enough. I think some of those scenes should have been written as Matt-and-George scenes."

Whatever feelings he may have about the individual episodes, Gary Graham points out that he enjoys the two-hour TV-movie format.

"I've worked in sitcoms, half-hour live audience, hour series, movies of the week, and features," he explains. "The feature pace is so slow, they've got so much money to spend and so much time to get all these little shots. As an actor, unless you're right there with the director, you just go to sleep. Your energy is just kind of dragging. Series pace is really breakneck, and after fifteen episodes you're really dragging, remembering lines from four episodes earlier. The sitcom, on the other hand, is very leisurely and fun. You show up, have coffee, crack jokes, suddenly you're having a rehearsal, then you go home at a decent hour, come back, do it for the producers, then the audience. It's fun-and-games time. I don't know how well I'm suited to that format, but it's a lot of fun.

"With the series, you make a lot of money but you really don't have a life. Your life is banging out the series. You try to decompress on the weekends, but by the time you start to relax and take a breath, it's time to go to work again. The only time to work out is 4:30 in the morning; the time to learn lines is when you get home and while you're eating dinner, then it's time to go to bed and get up and do it again. For nine or ten months you have no life. But the TV movie is a fast enough pace to keep you energized and slow enough to really get it right and discover the scene, as Kenny says. If we can keep banging out TV movies, I'd be a happy guy."

TVM 06. "THE CITY OF ANGELS"

Unproduced to date
Screenplay: Kenneth Johnson

Los Angeles is being torn apart by race riots between humans and the Tenctonese, and George Francisco finds himself in the eye of the storm. He is soon on trial for murder after a suspect responsible for severely wounding Buck dies during interrogation. Most shocking in the story line is the ultimate revelation that the riot may have been manufactured by and for several big businesses involved in the promotion of the Olympics.

Commentary

AUTHOR'S RATING of the Script Review: ***½

If produced, *City of Angels* will undoubtedly be a cross between the aftermath of the Rodney King trial and the O. J. Simpson courtroom spectacle. Unlike most TV series where a lead is charged with a crime and it's obvious from the outset that he (or she) will be freed, there are quite a few moments in this story line that raise serious questions about whether or not George will be found innocent by the court. Interestingly, no matter how the jury votes, George holds himself up to his own set of rules.

In fact, there is a wonderful court scene (in the script) where George gives a speech, which Eric Pierpoint will undoubtedly perform superbly. He says, in effect, that his primary purpose for being a police officer is to bring justice, not revenge, to the punishment of wrongdoers. (He had seen too much revenge and lawlessness aboard the ship where he and his people had been held as slaves.) However, in one blinding moment of rage and hatred, he let his desire for justice take the form of personal revenge at what he had seen done to his son and others. Therefore, he apologizes for his lapse and his ignoring of his primary responsibility as a law officer to see that justice is served impartially.

City of Angels will also mark a nice return for the Sikes character, whose past catches up with him. As racism is the governing factor of the riots and the trial, Sikes is censored for having been a bigot, often referring to the Tenctonese as Slags. Then, too, his inter-species relationship with Cathy is irritating to those around him. What is so meaningful about the opportunity this script offers Sikes is that he accepts his actions and mistakes of the past. He can now proudly proclaim that he has learned from his past errors and has evolved. Hopefully, there will be an opportunity to see Gary Graham work his acting magic on this challenging material.

THE FUTURE OF *ALIEN NATION*

Fox Broadcasting was apparently quite pleased with the ratings of the first three *Alien Nation* TV movies: *Dark Horizon, Body & Soul,* and *Millennium.* Indeed, the latter was dropped into the schedule on January 2 of 1995—not a high viewing day by any means—and scored more than a respectable audience. Unfortunately the fourth film, *The Enemy Within,* did poorly in the ratings when it aired in November of 1996 during sweeps, when it was pitted against powerhouse lineups on both the ABC and NBC networks. Fox Broadcasting looked at the ratings and came away with the conclusion that the viewing audience was no longer interested in *Alien Nation.* Thus, *The Udara Legacy* was "dumped" into the summer TV schedule.

Will *City of Angels,* or any other *Alien Nation* adventure, go into production? At this point, no one can be certain.

Despite this, everyone involved feels that if this is indeed the end of the series franchise, at least they were given the opportunity for closure, after the abrupt cancelation of the original weekly series, in a most satisfying way.

Eric Pierpoint philosophizes, "This is sort of like a Hollywood miracle. They gave us the bad news first, then they gave us the good news. If they had been forward-thinking enough at the time, we probably would have had a five-year run. But to actually be able to come back and do this has been great. When you're not done with a character, you feel so outraged that you have to leave him. As an actor, you feel violated somehow, that you've got more to say, more to do, that there is more life to breathe into these characters. Thankfully, we had that chance."

Costar Gary Graham assesses, "*Alien Nation* did some intelligent work. In a way, we're a series of signposts pointing the way to the future. In some shows, we're saying there are curves ahead, slow down. In others, we're saying, 'Warning! Stop and pay attention!' We worked very hard on it and had some good times. Who knows? If it flies again, by golly, I'll be right there in the co-pilot seat. If it doesn't, we had a hell of a ride."

Executive producer Ken Johnson, who has probably been more passionate about this show than any of his other considerable showbusiness credits, is quite pragmatic in his views of *The Udara Legacy* possibly being the final Tenctonese adventure. "If this ends up being the last one, we will all have gone out with our heads held high and very proud of the work that we have done," he says. "What *Alien Nation* does best is comment on ourselves and our society and, ultimately, hopefully, bring the races together so that we can see that our similarities are more important than our differences."

APPENDIX

A THE TENCTONESE FUNNIES

The Tenctonese are survivors. You may not think so, considering that *Alien Nation* was canceled after only one too-brief TV season, but they do indeed live on.

Besides the various reunion TV movies, there has also been a series of original novels from Pocket Books. In addition, Adventure Comics published a variety of comic mini-series between 1990 and 1992 which chronicled the adventures of Earth's future and the Newcomers' present. While contractually unable to use the characters of Sikes and Francisco, Adventure's writers utilized the premise to take an imaginative leap beyond the confines of the teleseries and the telemovies.

THE SPARTANS

Alien Nation: The Comics began with *The Spartans* (consisting of "Lost and Found", "Stone Walled", "Take Back the Stars", and "Death Dance"), the first mini-series to overcome the obstacle of not featuring the established characters as its focal point.

"I think many people wanted to see more of George and Matt," says writer Bill Spangler, "but I didn't feel particularly handicapped. The Newcomers represented a situation where something like their arrival would change so much about what's happening on Earth, that there were *all* kinds of ways to investigate it; all sorts of worthwhile stories that could be done.

"When I first started developing *The Spartans*," he adds, "I was told that Adventure wanted to keep seeing stories with a crime/mystery tone to them, but not necessarily another pair of cops. That was okay with me, because I couldn't do police procedural if my life depended on it. I did like some of the light mystery shows like *Remington Steele* [1982–87] and *The Scarecrow and Mrs. King* [1983–87], which is how we ended up with a man-woman pair in *The Spartans*."

In his four issues, Spangler dealt with a Purist (human supremacist) organization's attempts to prepare for a possible second "invasion" of Earth by the Tenctonese. To this end, they kidnap key members of the race and torture them to learn their technological secrets. Attempting to uncover the mystery is Newcomer FBI agent Justin Case and Newcomer Advocacy League member Ruth Lawrence.

"I didn't really want to do a story that created a new Tenctonese ritual or a new piece of biology," Spangler explains, "because I figured it would probably be invalidated by something that would come along in the TV series. So, I decided to concentrate on the human reactions to the Tenctonese presence. My wife and I were watching the show and she was talking about how the Tenctonese are so superior that it's understandable that some people might get scared about the human race's future. I took that as a jumping-off point for the Spartans' philosophy. The Spartans—this Purist group—had some serious questions to ask, but ended up taking this totally criminal and fanatical approach to get some answers."

In trying to analyze the ways in which Earth would react to the Tenctonese, Spangler developed a separate story line which he proposed to Pocket Books, though the story never made it to print.

"Would there be anything left for the comic book industry to think of if this science-fiction concept came into reality?" he asks rhetorically. "Would people want to read about superheroes and other types of fantasy presences? My proposal, called *The Rise and Fall of Captain Cosmos*, was about a human cartoonist who teams up with a Newcomer, and together they were going to be doing a graphic novel biography of the Newcomers. What would happen is that because the idea of a superhero is so similar to the Tenctonese version of a Guardian Angel, the Newcomer would eventually get a costume and start patrolling the streets. My point is that there are many different ways that this [the Newcomers' arrival] is going to be affecting this world—politically, sexually, in terms of sports—and many different things to investigate."

A BREED APART

A Sikes-Francisco-like police partnership was "reincarnated" in *A Breed Apart* (published between November 1990 and January 1991) in the form of human Wayne Hadenfeldt and Newcomer Log b'Omen, as they investigate a Tenctonese plot to use the cocaine trade to solidify a base of power.

"The inspiration," explains comic book writer Steve Jones, "was a class I took in college. I was taking a course on Asian culture, and we got into the opium wars—the whole idea of Britain bringing in opium to break the Chinese trade and China not wanting them there. I thought that would be interesting if, in *Alien Nation*, the bad guys would try to do the same thing. A character in the fourth issue says, 'Isn't this amazing? People were afraid that aliens were going to take over their world for years. Well, we're going to give it a shot, but not in a way that anyone would have imagined.'

"It's easy to take over the cocaine trade," he continues. "People would just get hooked on the stuff and society would just go downhill, which is almost what's going on in America right now. Certainly part of the culture is suffering from it. I wanted to explore that. Unfortunately, we didn't get a chance to do it because it was only four-issues long."

Jones admits that he's disappointed the series was so limited, particularly when he thought he would be *Alien Nation*'s regular writer. "Not to bring out dirty laundry," he says, "but originally I was called upon to write the series in four-issue increments. I could have an open plot line, but I should have an ending, even a loose one, every four issues. If you read the fourth issue of *A Breed Apart*, it's *really* open-ended. Too much so. What happened is that three-and-a-half issues through the story, I got this letter saying, 'The artist is slow, so we're going to let someone else jump ahead and do one of the other mini-series.' And I said, '*What* other mini-series? What is this?' But by then it was too late to finish this whole story line.

"I nonetheless think it's an interesting twist on what is a science-fiction cliché: Aliens landing and taking over Earth. I thought it would be interesting *not* to use ray guns, but something that already exists; something that's definitely affecting our society. It had a strong theme and would have been a strong story *if* we had gone with it."

THE SKIN TRADE

Inspired by such Humphrey Bogart excursions into *film noir* as *The Maltese Falcon* (1941), writer Lowell Cunningham developed private detective Mason Jar. In *The Skin Trade* (published between March and June 1991 and consisting of "The Case of the Missing Milksop", "To Live and Die in L.A.", "Big Trouble in Little Tencton", and "The Big Goodbye"), Jar is searching for a woman's missing husband when he comes upon a plot in which criminal Newcomers are being surgically altered to look human (and vice versa) to avoid prosecution. His opponents throughout are Dexter Methorophan and his henchmen Graham Cracker and Kayo Pectate.

"When I began thinking of a story," Cunningham details, "I got in the habit of playing word games, because the aliens have unusual names. Any place that I saw something that could have turned into a name, I did it. If I drove by a garden shop, I would think 'Pete Moss.' Then I saw a nasal spray commercial and I got Dexter Methorophan. I was in a grocery store shopping, saw a Mason jar, and thought that was a good name. I envisioned a cheap detective—a Newcomer—and the series grew around that idea. Dexter Methorophan sounded like a really heavy guy, so I made him the bad guy. The story worked around the genre. I had to find some conflict that would be appropriate to the background and that's where *The Skin Trade* aspect came in."

In terms of developing Mason's particular vocation and the fact that he very much dresses the part, Cunningham notes, "In the background of the film and TV series, the aliens were kept in quarantine. I reasoned that they were there to be taught or entertained or both, and I figured that they probably watched a lot of TV and old movies. So, Mason sees movies like *The Maltese Falcon* and it fascinates him, because he has been a slave all his life, yet here's this character who's facing enormous odds and able to stay his own man. That would be a powerful image for somebody who had just come out of slavery.

"I wrote a scene in the series where Mason talks about watching the movie. He didn't know what a detective was, but that's what he wanted to be as soon as he got out; that's why he dresses that way and acts like a man out of time. He's fitting that image and it makes him look a little eccentric. At the same time, the other aliens coming to him as clients would have no perception of what a *real* detective would be except the same source that he has. They see him as someone fitting in, even though humans see him as a little weird."

Cunningham returned to the realm of *Alien Nation* with *Public Enemy* (published between December 1991 and March 1992, and consisting of "Before the Fall", "Fallen Angels", "Vengeance is Mine", and "Angel of Death"). "The title character is John Q. Public and he's fortunate to have been given that name because it has given him lots of jobs to do in advertising," he laughs. "Everyone wants to have John Q. Public in their advertising, so *Public Enemy* is a play on that. This series is quite a bit different than *The Skin Trade.*

"One thing I did was have the first issue take place entirely on the slave ship, which no one has ever done before. It's not so much a flashback as a prologue, and it features a group of characters who are immune to this gas that's enslaving everyone. The first issue shows what their life is like and what they're doing about the time the ship crashed on Earth. The rest of the story involves what happens several years later."

Another difference between the two comic book "mini-series," as Cunningham sees it, is the fact that Mason Jar is something of a square peg in a round hole; someone who doesn't quite fit in. John Q. Public, conversely, fits in "a little too well, to the point where he's accused by one of his friends of practically being a human," Cunningham states. "They don't like that and he doesn't like that. But because of his name getting him all these commercials, he has become an icon. He's the ultimate Newcomer, fitting into society on his own terms. We find out that Newcomers call other Newcomers 'John Q' as an insult. He isn't aware of that because he's removed from having to face the problems that the average Newcomer must face. That's the personal conflict he has, and the physical conflict is that there's somebody out there trying to kill him and succeeding in killing many people close to him."

He believes that not being able to work with the Sikes and Francisco characters wasn't as difficult as one would think. "The fascination for me," he says, "is seeing these aliens who represent every minority, whatever minority you want to choose. Seeing them interact with a society that we feel more familiar with is a way to make commentary that you don't have to have a set character to make. It's more effective if you're familiar with a character and can experience things with them, but I think it nonetheless works without them."

APE NATION

The most unusual *Alien Nation* comic book "mini-series" was undoubtedly *Ape Nation* (published in 1991), a crossover title with Adventure's *Planet of the Apes*, written by Charles Marshall.

An off-the-cuff office joke resulted in this tale in which the Newcomer slave ship transcends the time barrier to crash on Earth in the far future. Once there, the Overseers decide to team up with the intelligent gorillas and an army of humans to take over the world.

"The success of [Dark Horse Comics'] *ALIEN vs. Predator* was definitely a factor that made them at least look at the idea seriously," explains Marshall. "I think many people looked at the idea as a rip-off of that, but I thought we pulled it off pretty well. In a way, I liked it better than anything else I had worked on. It seemed to bring across the right mix of adventure and humor, and I thought the artwork was stunning. Coming up with the story wasn't difficult, though I was intent on making sure that the vehicle to get the two groups together wasn't just waxed over. I really hit the books and tried to come up with a time-travel idea that was, in some ways, plausible."

For Marshall, the appeal of *Alien Nation* was the complex interaction between the characters of Sikes and Francisco, which is something he tried to capture in *Ape Nation* using his own protagonists. "What this mini-series tries to do is pick up some of that same appeal, except that instead of being a human, the other character is an ape. These two characters develop a buddy relationship much like *Alien Nation*.

"The way I look at it," he adds, "is that you have this slave race. There are *no* resources being harvested on the planet of the apes and there's *nothing* for these slaves to do, so I figured that it would be a logical offshoot that they would be used for the only job open, an army. So, they're part of this vast army that's wiping out everything on the way to Ape City. Basically, though, it's the story of two characters. The ape's name is Heston, and it's pretty obvious that came from [Charlton Heston, who starred in 1968's *Planet of the Apes*]. The alien is Caan, which I thought was a nice tribute to James Caan [Sykes in the original *Alien Nation* feature film]. I've tried to pick up the buddy quality that appealed to me about *Alien Nation* and work that in too.

"I've always been a fan of weird crossovers, and it's a challenge to pull it off and not have people say, 'Oh, that's the *dumbest* thing I've ever heard.' The idea isn't as far-fetched as it sounds. I thought that they almost complemented each other. In a way, I felt it worked *better* than *ALIEN vs. Predator*."

THE FIRSTCOMERS

Like *Ape Nation*, Martin Powell's *The FirstComers* (published between May and August 1991) tackles *Alien Nation* from a slightly different vantage point.

"I had pretty much heard and read about what everyone else was doing and it all sounded to me like the movie," says the writer. "So I thought, 'There has to be something else we could do.' The more I thought about it, the more I started to consider what has become a modern myth. There's this rumor that in 1947 a flying saucer crashed somewhere in Mexico and it was taken to this mysterious Hangar 18 Air Force base. The information was released to newspapers—I have Xeroxes of microfilms of this—that the United States Air Force had captured a flying saucer. It was published in the *New York Times*.

"Then, the very next day, they recanted and said it was actually a weather balloon. To me, the most ominous aspect was that they invited the press the first day. Pictures of the debris shown were taken. The very next day, when they decided that it was a weather balloon, some of the same photographers were there and noticed that the material being shown was different. Most of these people, including some high-ranking army officials, have come out over the past few years and admitted that they didn't know what it was.

"The more I got into it, the stranger it got," Powell continues. "There definitely seems to be something going on. It seems like many otherwise very reasonable people are risking a great deal to their reputations and careers to say that some really strange things are happening. I thought, 'What a great idea for a story.'"

Powell postulated a scenario in which, despite the fact that mankind has accepted the Newcomers, the events of Hangar 18 are still a secret. Why?

"That's the basis of the story," he smiles. "It has been over fifty years their time—it takes place in 1997—and it's still being very carefully guarded, and people who know about it are dying. The main character, Jack Wotts, has been following this particular story for years. Finally, he manages to break into a government compound and steals a file, then dead bodies start popping up every place he goes as they start looking for him. He inadvertently gets thrown together with this Newcomer woman who hates his guts, because he's like a modern Bogart character. He's very cynical, though his heart, as it turns out, is in the right place, but he can never find it. He's a real obnoxious jerk for the most part. He's not a Purist in the true sense of the word: he hates *everybody* equally. So, they end up going to the root of this, to people he has been corresponding with for years, and they start getting killed."

"It's more of an investigative kind of detective story with a very eerie mystery, almost supernatural in nature. The mystery of what's going on is what I follow. In terms of the FirstComers and who they are, where they came from, you never know. Overall, I really wanted to give a feeling—and this is something the TV series lacked sometimes—of living in a different culture on the planet Earth. Imagine living completely away from human beings and you know that things are going to be viewed in drastically different ways. It's bound to be. I never found it that much on *Alien Nation*. It seemed to me in most cases that the aliens were quite human, oftentimes more human than the human characters.

"*FirstComers* is really a science-fiction detective story," he says. "There's none of the cops-and-robbers material, though there is a stalking killer through the series whose identity hopefully was a big surprise. I very much enjoyed doing it. It was a different kind of experience for me, and unlike *anything* I had ever written before."

If nothing else, the Adventure Comics line proved that while the original TV series didn't last very long, the *ideals* of *Alien Nation* have lived on.

"Outside the good premise, writing, acting, and Kenneth Johnson's guiding the whole thing," offers Steve Jones in terms of the series' enduring appeal, "they took the time to develop this alien culture, to think about it and bring it to us week by week, bit by bit. They said, 'This is what these people are like. This is how they look at us and how we look at them. Let's get to know them and maybe learn a little bit about ourselves.'"

The lessons continue.

APPENDIX B NOVELS

Several years after the cancelation of *Alien Nation*, Pocket Books launched a series of novels which continued the saga. What follows is a brief overview of these fictions:

1. *THE DAY OF DESCENT*

Written by Judith and Garfield Reeves Stevens   Publication Date: March 1993

A prequel to both the feature film and the television series. Matthew Sikes is a rookie cop, going about his usual business, when reports filter through of an approaching spacecraft. It is only a matter of time before the Tenctonese arrive on Earth, affecting the world in general and Sikes in particular.

2. *DARK HORIZON*

Written by K. W. Jeter   Publication Date: August 1993

A novelization of the *Alien Nation* episode "Green Eyes" (TVS 22), as well as the then-unproduced two-hour teleplay *Dark Horizon* (TVM 01), in which the Tenctonese battle for their very lives against a viral threat from the Purists. At the same time, the Newcomer Ahpossno arrives on Earth, the scout for the slaves' former masters who has come to retrieve their property and the rest of humanity as a bonus.

3. *BODY & SOUL*

Written by Peter David   Publication Date: December 1993

A novelization of the second two-hour TV movie, unproduced at the time of publication, chronicling the efforts of Sikes and Cathy to take their relationship to the next step, and at the same time dealing with the arrival of both a giant and infant Newcomer who are intricately connected and are the results of a bizarre Tenctonese experiment.

4. *THE CHANGE*

Written by Barry B. Longyear Publication Date: March 1994

This novel was based on an unproduced teleplay written for *Alien Nation*'s aborted second season. George Francisco begins a physical change common to the Tenctonese which could threaten his life. At the same time, he must cope with a killer from his past who is after him and his family.

5. *SLAG LIKE ME*

Written by Barry B. Longyear Publication Date: July 1994

When a journalist who has gone undercover as a Newcomer to learn firsthand about racism in Los Angeles disappears, it's up to Sikes and George to find out what happened. In the ultimate irony, Sikes is in the position of having to become a Tenctonese himself in order to uncover the truth and learn something about himself along the way.

6. *PASSING FANCY*

Written by David Spencer Publication Date: December 1994

A woman from Sikes's past shows up, leading him and George into an investigation of a new drug that is sweeping Los Angeles, with deadly results. En route, and because of this woman, the two police officers find the tensions between them getting worse than usual.

7. *EXTREME PREJUDICE*

Written by L. A. Graf Publication Date: March 1995

When Sikes and George are sent to Pittsburgh, they become involved in a homicide case that turns out to be much more than what it seems on the surface. Indeed, the killer may well turn out to be otherworldly.

8. *CROSS OF BLOOD*

Written by K. W. Jeter Publication Date: July 1995

Definitely going where the series had *not* gone before, *Cross of Blood* presents Cathy getting pregnant with Sikes's child, and the resultant birth of the first Tenctonese-human hybrid divides Los Angeles. Sikes can't even depend on George, who has quit the police force to join a mysterious cult with which he has become obsessed.

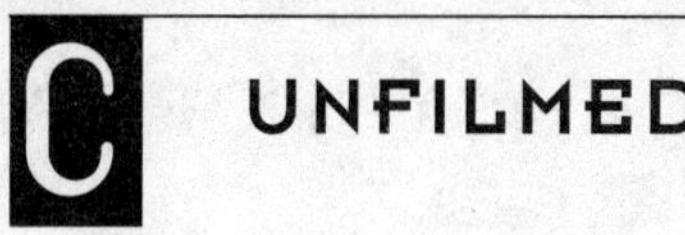

APPENDIX C UNFILMED

ON SEPARATE WAYS

Writer: Tom Chehak
Status: Unproduced teleplay for the TV series

A succession of Tenctonese child kidnappings leads Sikes, George, and Cathy to Paris where they discover that the youngsters are being sold on the black market and that something in their blood is poisonous to humans.

Back home, George and Susan wonder if the children are suffering from the same virus that infected young Tenctonese on the Landing Three Mining Camp, where the couple attempted to shield the young ones from the Overseers who would kill them at the first sign of weakness.

Cathy eventually learns that the children are going through a Predeal Effect, an odor given off by the body to ward off predators but which, because of the carbon monoxide of Earth's atmosphere, is becoming toxic. The only cure, as far as she can determine, is for them to be reunited with their mothers to drink their milk and, thus, return to normal.

Sikes and George are eventually led to baby broker Mr. Salamandra, who has been in the business of selling infants since the late 1970s. George and Susan are so desperate to stop Salamandra that they come up with a plan by which they will use Vessna as bait, offering to put her up for sale. Sikes is against the idea, but George insists it's the only way to get Salamandra. The sting proves to be successful.

Back at the police station, George invites Sikes over to his home for dinner, but he declines. Instead, Sikes meets with Cathy, who tells him that the recovered infants are now back to normal. To celebrate, they dine at a French restaurant.

APPENDIX

TENCTONESE ENCYCLOPEDIA

Compiled by Pete Chambers

A longstanding tradition in science fiction is creating an alien language to help differentiate such cultures from humanity. Most of the time, these so-called "languages" are merely a series of grunts. But, as is the case with the Klingons on the various *Star Trek* spin-offs, the producers of *Alien Nation* decided that for the Tenctonese language to be effective, there actually had to be some logic to it. What follows is a breakdown of key Tenctonese phrases that have been utilized in the TV series and TV movies.

A

AKLA FLUID: Newcomer sperm.
ANDARKO: Male half of the Celinist Tenctonese religious diad.
ATROPHICATION: Chemical change in the Newcomer body.
AXILLA: The particularly sensitive nerve cluster in the armpits of Newcomers. A hit there has an effect similar to a blow to the testicles of a human. A severe blow, with enough accuracy, can be fatal.

B

BAH/NA FLUID: Newcomer seminal fluid.
BAKKO: Newcomer ball game played on courts.
BIN YIN OIL: Oil used during pod ejection.
BINNAUM: The third Newcomer sex, similar to the male, who supplies catalyzing emission during procreation. Binnaums tend to have larger head-spot markings. Albert Einstein is a Binnaum.
BOLENITHIS DISEASE: A very contagious Newcomer disease which also affects humans.

C

CARPUZAL GLANDS: Newcomer facial glands.

CAVES OF TENCTON: An underground meeting place used in ancient Tenctonese society. A replica is made in the episode "Gimme, Gimme" (TVS 20).

CELENITIPRA: Matriarchal Newcomer religious system.

CELINE: Female half of the Celinist Tenctonese religious diad.

CELINITI: Tenctonese religion.

CHEERBUSHA: A spider-web-like cocoon where young children are placed, surrounded by loved ones but isolated, protected, for eleven months to harmonize the senses.

CHEKKAH: Elite Newcomer Overseer reconnaissance unit.

CHERBOKE: Doctor who performed horrific experiments on the *Gruza* slave ship.

CHOOKLAK: Love nest.

CLICK: The Click is used in several ways by the Tenctonese. It is used as a punctuation and extra character in their language. In the pilot episode, George is seen in the warehouse, clicking to aid his sense of smell, possibly indicating the presence of a cat-like "Jacobson's organ," giving an increased sense of taste and smell.

CLOT STO LEAKIAN DISEASE: Newcomer bone disorder.

CYTERIAN GLANDS: Newcomer glands that produce the enzymes Bardok, Rosto, and Yunosi (also called Unost).

D

DAROK: Newcomer gift of friendship.

DAY OF DESCENT: Newcomer holiday celebrating their arrival on Earth (supposedly October 19, 1990).

DINAR: Ceremonial covering cloth for daroks and Tenctonese chests.

DORK: Revered one; the "being" of honor for the Day of Descent holiday.

DREGNA: Usually a derogatory Overseer's term for slaves, but actually means "cargo."

DREVNI: An elder in the order of Binnaum.

DROONAL FLANGES: Newcomer head glands.

DROONAL FLANGE BRUSH: Brush used for cleaning droonal flanges.

E

EEMIKKEN: A "no gas" tablet that counteracts the effects of the "Holy Gas" used to control the slaves.

EENOS: Cannibalistic Newcomer outcasts. The lowest of the low, Eenos have gray, ill-defined spots.

ELDERS: When on the ship, the Elders acted as a sort of secret government in exile. Here on Earth they are still consulted and held in esteem. Uncle Moodri was an Elder.

F

FLUPTEL: Newcomer male enzyme.

G

GAHSAC: Newcomer male menopause.

GANNAUM: Main Newcomer male sex who fertilizes during procreation. George, Buck, and Moodri are all Gannaums. (See *Haffacota*, below.)

GLAHEB: Newcomer embalming fluid.

GLEENY GLANDS: Newcomer glands located under the armpits.

GRUZA: The name of the Tenctonese slave ship that crashed on Earth.

H

HAFFACOTA: Embryonic pod carried by the Linnaum (Tenctonese female) for the first half of the pregnancy before being transferred to the Gannaum (male) for the second half of the pregnancy.

HO/LODKA: Drug used to lower temperature in the Tenctonese body.

HOLY GAS: Gas used on the slave ship to subdue the slaves.

HOVED RAKSTAFS: Newcomer erogenous gland of the back.

HUMMER: Humming of the spots—Newcomer foreplay.

I

IONIA: Goddess of Celenitipra religious system.

J

JOURNEY STONE: A small, polished stone given to the traveler to bring good luck.

K

KA/NA DRUM: Tenctonese ceremonial drum. Played by Emily to the annoyance of everyone else and acting as a catalyst for Matt's amusing and revealing nightmare scene in the novel version and original script of "Body & Soul" (TVM 02).

KAIF BALLS: Felt balls containing aromatic and therapeutic Tenctonip or Nunip, which has a similar effect on the Tenctonese as catnip has on cats.

KARABLA: Decorative wedding altar in the shape of a ceremonial boat (for the new journey together) into which the happy couple take their Serdso during the wedding.

KLOKHLA/TULYA: Newcomer male hormone.

KRONTLE KRAW: Like goose bumps.

KUMLEKULA: Newcomer disease like pneumonia.

L

LING-POD FLAP: Part of the stomach-pod pouch of male Newcomers.

LINNAUM: Newcomer female sex who carries the haffacota or embryonic pod until it is transferred to the male halfway through the pregnancy. Susan, Cathy, Emily, and Vessna are all Linnaums.

LITTLE TENCTON: Slum area of Los Angeles, where many of the Tenctonese live.

LUIBOF: Tenctonese spiritual religious cult.

M

MATA: Newcomer glands located near the spine, which control puberty.

MILAC: Ether-like chemical (sometimes also called orkas).

MOOCTEEBUTI: Newcomer christening-like ceremony.

N

NABAROTE: Newcomer breech birth (Vessna was nabarote).

NEELEXES: Long-armed sticks, netted at one end and clubbed at the other, used in the team game Zepro.

NEESTAS: Puberty.

NOKLICK'S SYNDROME: A rather rare Newcomer disease which affects one out of a hundred thousand. The nitrogen-hydrogen ratio of the Earth's atmosphere affects respiratory function and the spinal column.

NOUVAN BOEN RANGE: A group of slave colonies where the Tenctonese aboard the Gruza worked.

O

ODDYASH WHEEL: Baby's play wheel.

ORKAS: Ether-like chemical (more often called milac).

OSCILLATOR: Turntable for Newcomer babies, good for the harmony of their being and also used as a pacifier.

P

PALACH: Gladiatorial-like sport contested between two club-wielding fighters.

PAPAYA: Collective sense of doom, said to be experienced by the Tenctonese before the coming of the slave ships.

POD: Newcomer fetus encased in a shell, ejected by the female and carried by the male.

POKHORONA: Celenist funeral-like ceremony.

POLAHANAHAMA SYNDROME: Mumps-like disease.

PORTAL: A Tenctonese box which is regarded as a religious icon. The box has the ability to generate a virtual-reality world that is in sympathy with the user's mood and expectations.

POTNIKI SPOTS: Newcomer back spots. These are an erogenous zone and can provoke a strong reaction if not treated with respect, as Matt finds out when he kisses Cathy's potniki spots in *Body & Soul* (TVM 02).

PREDEAL: Protective poisonous slime, excreted by Newcomer baby deprived of Yespian (mother's milk).

PURISTS: Human quasi-fascist group dedicated to fighting Tenctonese emancipation. The more extreme members want the total destruction of the aliens.

Q

QUA-HIB: Tenctonese embalming fluid. A sweet preparation to aid the departed on the way to Celine.

R

RAZVITI HORMONE: Hormone given off by pregnant Newcomer females, which is very arousing to Newcomer males.

RELIGIONS: The Tenctonese have several religions. The Franciscos are Celinists, who follow the teachings of Andarko and Celine; Uncle Moodri was a Celenitipra, a religion which is matriarchal in its belief; and Cathy is a member of a Buddhist-like religion.

ROOKPLATCH: Tenctonese skin disorder, brought on by stress.

S

SANDISKA: Mineral once mined by the Tenctonese slaves.

SARDONAC: Newcomer aphrodisiac and bonding drug.

SEE HAMTHA: The touch; the touching of temples (love is received through the touching of temples).

SELEB: Tenctonese blessing.

SEMYA CHAIN: Metal chain, each link of which is made by the previous generation and handed down to the next.

SERDSO: Octagonal-shaped crystal ornament owned by all Tenctonese; legend has it the Serdso contains the owner's soul. Duels were once fought over them.

SLAG: Abusive slang term for the Tenctonese.

SLAGTOWN: Slang name for "Little Tencton," the slum area of Los Angeles where most of the Tenctonese live.

SLEEPER HOLD: Applying pressure underneath the ear valleys of a Newcomer will cause them to black out. George uses this hold on Cathy in *Dark Horizon* (TVM 01) and on the giant in *Body & Soul* (TVM 02).

SONAH: Newcomer psychological condition of having no self; still having a slave mentality.

SPARTIARY GLAND: Gland which regulates Newcomer metabolism.

SPECIAL SECTION: The area of the slave ship where Cherboke and Vesant conducted their experiments.

SPOROT: Baby-holding cradle used for Moocteebuti ceremony.

SS'JABROKA: Drug used originally in the slave mining colonies to reward and control the Tenctonese. When taken in large quantities it produces a frightening change in the aliens. Their size and musculature increase, the skin becomes hard and scaly, the skull swollen with razor-sharp fangs. Alternate spellings used in the *Alien Nation* novels are *jabroka* and *zhabrokah*.

T

TADLIN: A green worm-like creature that was a popular food treat with Tenctonese children on the slave ship.

TAGDOT: Mythical, nightmarish warrior of legend who slew his foes by severing their hands and leaving them to bleed to death. He is recalled in the Halloween-like "The Night of Screams" (TVS 07).

TAJELLO GLANDS: Hormone-producing glands.

TENCTON: The home planet of the Tenctonese race.

TENCTONESE: Alien slave race now living free on Earth. The Tenctonese look generally similar to humans, but have no hair. Instead, they have large spot-like markings on their heads and down their spines. The aliens are thirty percent stronger and twenty percent smarter than the average human. Tenctonese is also the name of the language spoken by the aliens.

TENCTRAN: The Tenctonese translator computer program.

TERRAS: Newcomer Day of Descent beads.

TERT: Newcomer derogatory term for human.

THACTAZOID SPOTTING: Line-shaped spotting on head or back.

TUNDASH: A village on Tencton.

U

UDARA: Newcomer samurai-like warrior. They waged a terrorist campaign against the Overseers on the ship.

V

VADAMICHI: Ritual wedding bath.

VENDA CRYSTALS: Colored crystals, given by the Luibof cult to bring comfort.

VESANT: Cherboke's best surgeon and chief accomplice.

VESSEL OF CELINE: Ornate bowl used to hold the family's gifts for a Moocteebuti.

VYDAK: Name of the pod-transferring ceremony.

W

WOJCHEK: Tenctonese Russian roulette wheel, which sprays a jet of salt water onto the chest of the unlucky loser.

Y

YDERON: Tenctonese colony.

YESPIAN: Mother's milk.

Z

ZABEET: Fourth-class citizen in old Tenctonese class society. Usually of lower intelligence.

ZEPRO: Tenctonese team game played with Neelexes.

APPENDIX

ACTOR BIOGRAPHIES

GARY GRAHAM (DETECTIVE MATTHEW SIKES)

In this actor's capable hands, Detective Matthew Sikes evolved from a human bigot towards the Tenctonese to, as the actor calls it, a "friend to Newcomers" between the original run of *Alien Nation* and the TV reunion movies several years later.

Born in Long Beach, California, Graham grew up in Orange County and attended the University of California, Irvine, where he studied both pre-med and drama. When he decided to switch to acting, he was stunned by what he was required to do. "They said I had to take dance," he laughs. "And I said, 'What? Put on those tights? Are you kidding?' But I started doing it and suddenly I realized, 'Hey, this is art. This isn't easy at all.' Dance was a very hard discipline. Then I tried ballet and was suddenly surrounded by beautiful women...and it was great."

His dancing in a college production of *Kiss Me, Kate* led him to a dancing job in the chorus of the San Diego Ballet's *Romeo and Juliet*. This was followed by a dancing and acting stint at Sebastian's West Dinner Playhouse, the success of which propelled him into the West Coast premiere of Lanford Wilson's *The Mound Builders*.

He began in feature films in Paul Schrader's *Hardcore* (1979), followed a year later by the comedy *Hollywood Knights*. This, in turn, was followed by a costarring role as Tom Cruise's brother in 1983's *All the Right Moves*, and roles in the 1991 sci-fi feature *Robojox* and 1993's *Necronomicon*. On television he played a hit man in an early episode of the Bruce Willis-Cybill Shepherd series, *Moonlighting* (1985–89), portrayed Brett Butler's date in an episode of *Grace Under Fire* (1993–98), and has guest-starred on *Hunter* (1984–91), *The Commish* (1991–95), *Renegade* (1992–), *Remington Steele* (1982–87), and *Star Trek: Voyager* (1995–). He also had a recurring role on *M.A.N.T.I.S.* (1994–95) as Captain Ken Hetrick.

His TV movie credits include *Fire on the Mountain* (1981), *No Place to Hide* (1981), *Thou Shalt Not Kill* (1982), *Money on the Side* (1982), *The Dirty Dozen: The Deadly Mission* (1987), *In the Best Interest of the Children* (1992), and *Trouble Shooters: Trapped Beneath the Earth* (1993).

Concerning *Alien Nation*'s character Matt Sikes, Graham notes, "Sikes is a cop because, number one, he loves it. Number two, he just can't see himself doing anything else. He's a rule breaker, but he gets the job done. Instinctual, compulsive...the type of guy I'd want to go into battle with—a knee-jerk kind of guy."

ERIC PIERPOINT (DETECTIVE GEORGE FRANCISCO)

Tenctonese police officer George Francisco has probably had more to do with the humanizing of Matt Sikes than anyone else, with George learning a thing or two from his partner as well.

The son of former CBS Washington, D.C., correspondent Robert Pierpoint, Eric grew up in the nation's capitol and can actually recall flying on the presidential press plane in the late 1960s. It wasn't until 1977 that he began seriously pursuing his acting dream, joining the National Players touring company, which took classical theater "on the road," performing Shakespeare throughout the United States. "We hit every small theatre from New York to Denver," he says. "Real grass-roots theater. We performed for an audience of fourteen nuns in New Orleans, and nearly two thousand terrifying teenagers in Arkansas. I got a terrific education doing that."

Pierpoint appeared off-Broadway in *Dangerous Corner, The Gingham Dog,* and in the American premiere of *Joseph and the Amazing Technicolor Dreamcoat.* With the Harke Theatre, he portrayed Stanley in *A Streetcar Named Desire,* Theseus in *A Midsummer Night's Dream,* and the title role of Sly in *Sly Fox.*

His film credits include *Windy City* (1984), *Invaders from Mars* (1986), and *Forever Young* (1992). On television, he has guest-starred in *Beauty and the Beast, In the Heat of the Night* (1988–94), *Silk Stalkings* (1991–), *Star Trek: The Next Generation* (1987–94), *Star Trek: Deep Space Nine* (1993–), and *Time Trax* (1993–94). He had recurring roles in *Fame* (1982–87), and costarred in 1984's *Hot Pursuit* (which was produced by Ken Johnson) as Jim Wyler, who, along with his wife, was on the lam from authorities for a murder they didn't commit. He also portrayed a cameraman in the drama *WIOU* (1990–91).

As Pierpoint will readily explain, he truly enjoys playing George Francisco on *Alien Nation*, offering this description of the character: "He wants the respect of his peers and hopes to be accepted for who he is, a humble alien who is secure in his own identity. He's a well-disciplined employee who is just trying to work his way up the ladder. George carries himself with an inner-confidence while adapting to his new surroundings. Even though he approaches his new lifestyle with curiosity, George is comfortable with who he is and can tolerate virtually all obstacles directed toward him. It's his self-confidence that's the key to George's strength."

MICHELE SCARABELLI (SUSAN FRANCISCO)

Keeping the Francisco family sane seems to be the objective of Susan Francisco, wife to George and mother to Buck, Emily, and Vessna.

Besides appearing in numerous commercials, the Montreal, Canada, native Scarabelli has been seen in such American television series as *Beverly Hills, 90210* (1990–), *Dudley* (1993), *Dallas* (1978–91), and *Star Trek: The Next Generation* (in which she portrayed an *Enterprise* crew member in love with the android Data). She has starred in the Canadian series *Okavango* and *FLTRRI*, as well as USA-Cable's *Air Wolf II*, in which she portrayed Jo Santini in the show's only season (1987). TV movie credits include *Perry Mason, A Month of Sundays, The Ruling Passion, Labor of Love, Age-Old Friends, The Colony,* and *The Wrong Woman*. She can be seen in the features *Hotel New Hampshire* (1984), *I Don't Buy Kisses Anymore* (1992), and *Dead Bolt* (1995), as well as numerous television commercials.

"Susan, George, and the others are basically idealized human beings who can be manipulated by whatever the writers see as issues that need to be addressed," says Scarabelli of *Alien Nation*. "But, because these are beings from another planet, we can take these issues and throw the audience a curveball. The show has constantly shifted textures and tones. And that's great for the actors because it allows us the opportunity to give in each episode."

TERRI TREAS (CATHY FRANKEL)

Whenever there's a need for a scientist or doctor, Matt and George turn to Newcomer Dr. Cathy Frankel, who also happens to be Sikes's girlfriend.

Cathy's real-life alter ego, Terri Treas, began her career in the theater in such shows as *Pal Joey, Pippin, Dancin'*, and *Working*. She followed these stints with performances in the films *The Best Little Whorehouse in Texas* (1984), *The Nest* (1988), *The Fabulous Baker Boys* (1989), and *House Party IV* (1995).

Born in Kansas City, Missouri, Treas has also appeared in the TV series *Nothing in Common* (1987), *Murphy Brown* (1988–), *Jake and the Fatman* (1987–92), and *Simon and Simon* (1981–88). More recently she directed the feature *Play Nice* (1992) and is a story editor on USA-Cable's *Silk Stalkings.*

"I've taken a lot from my own experience and put it into the character of Cathy," Treas says. "The thing that is the closest parallel between Cathy and myself is that, as a woman functioning in a very high-pressure career, we've both had to develop a certain kind of behavior that appears to be very competent, capable, and strong. But, in Cathy's case, that doesn't mean she has the same emotional equipment. That's where my own polarity comes into play. I feel very sensitive and vulnerable as a human being and I've infused those elements into Cathy. Her situation is quite different from mine. She's vulnerable and innocent. She has been very sheltered. But I feel my own real-life insecurities fit in well with this character."

SEAN SIX (BUCK FRANCISCO)

Sean Six's Buck Francisco has gone through an interesting evolution from the beginning of the TV series—where he thought his father was a sell-out for working with the humans—to the more recent *Alien Nation* TV movie, *The Udara Legacy* (1997), where he has joined the police academy.

A native of New York City, Six began his career working in a production of *Fiddler on the Roof* at the San Francisco Civic Auditorium. He got his big break in the play *Riff*, followed by the lead in a Los Angeles production of *Spring Awakening*. He costarred in the features *Thirteen* and *Rough Trade* and the TV films *The Iceman Cometh* and *To My Daughter.* He had a recurring role in the 1988 TV series *Something Is Out There.*

"Buck Francisco," says Sean, "is a teenager who is trying to connect with something, but the truth he connects with isn't the right one.

The whole teenage thing is about finding out who you are. Buck is doing just that...trying to relate to something—his parents, his friends, anything. It's something all of us can identify with."

LAUREN WOODLAND (EMILY FRANCISCO)

From the original TV series through the made-for-television *Alien Nation* movies, Lauren Woodland has literally grown up before America's eyes as the daughter of George and Susan Francisco.

Besides starring in *The Dom DeLuise Show* (1987–88), Lauren has appeared in TV's *Brooklyn Bridge* (1991–93), *L.A. Law* (1986–94), *Quantum Leap* (1989–93), *St. Elsewhere* (1982–88), and *The Judge* (1986–92), as well as in over forty commercials. Her films include *Body Count, Super Star, Cover-Up* (1991), and *Frame Up* (1991), and she has performed with the Joffrey Ballet in such productions as *The Nutcracker* and *Romeo and Juliet*.

"Emily is one of those characters that seems to be able to go anywhere," says Woodland. "She's far from being the stereotypical little sister. Emily is as average as a kid on this show can be. She's not your typical Earth kid with a different look, but during the show she does seem to be experiencing some of the same problems Earth kids have. Emily, in a sense, is confused. She wants to be cool and she wants to fit in—just like human children. But at the same time, she's intent on preserving her alien heritage."

JEFF MARCUS (ALBERT EINSTEIN)

The seemingly dim-witted precinct janitor, Albert Einstein, has turned out to be much more than that as *Alien Nation* has continued its on-air saga.

Jeff Marcus, who portrays Albert, studied at Carnegie-Mellon University, where he performed extensive studies in acting, voice, speech, and dance. On stage he has costarred in *As You Like It, Short Change, Meeting the Winter Bikerider, Hot and Cold*, and *Almost an Eagle*. His television credits include the TV movies *Family Business, Playing for Time* (1980), *Senior Trip* (1981), *Eleanor: First Lady of the World* (1982), and *The 13th Floor* (1988), as well as the feature films *Endless Love* and *The Chosen* (both 1981), *Promised Land* (1988), and *When Tomorrow Hits* (1990).

"Albert has a vulnerability about him that I enjoy working with," says Marcus. "I think everybody has this trait in common, but Albert hasn't been tooled enough to conceal it. He is really the child in me who knows when to flash a warm smile and project that lovable side to get attention, he just has a harder time pulling it off with that oversized alien head."

RON FASSLER (CAPTAIN BRYAN GRAZER)

Although he initially didn't do more on the TV series than give Sikes and George their assignments or reprimand them, Ron Fassler's Captain Grazer has developed into a sound leader who assesses the public relations and/or fiscal opportunities of the cases that come the way of his squad.

Fassler has appeared on the television programs *Beverly Hills, 90210* (1990–), *Living Single* (1993–97), *The Fresh Prince of Bel-Air* (1990–97), *St. Elsewhere* (1982–88), and *L.A. Law* (1986–94), as well as the films *Gremlins II* (1990), *Child's Play III* (1991), and *Camp Nowhere* (1994). Additionally, he starred in the Los Angeles premiere of the Broadway comedy *Lend Me a Tenor*, and can be seen in many television commercials.

APPENDIX

ON THE INTERNET

Alien Nation also exists in cyberspace, with several network sites and an appreciation society with worldwide membership. This society is known as "The *Alien Nation* Appreciation Society—The Tencton Planet." Its president is Pete Chambers and the vice president is Connie Colvin, with Kenneth Johnson (executive producer of the TV series and the TV movies), Eric Pierpoint (who played George Francisco in the series), Lauren Woodland (who played Emily Francisco, George's daughter, in the series), Jeff Marcus (who played Albert Einstein, the Newcomer janitor, in the series), Craig Binkley (property master for the TV series), and Venila Ozols-Graham (associate producer for the TV series and the TV movies) as honorary members.

The world contacts for the Society are as follows:

1. THE TENCTON PLANET (United Kingdom and the rest of the world): 110 Richmond Street, Coventry, CV2 4HY, UK.
2. THE TENCTON PLANET (United States of America): 32-21 87th Street, Jackson Heights, New York, NY 11369-2137, USA.
3. THE TENCTON PLANET (Australia): 11 Morris Court, Springvale North, Victoria 3171, Australia.
4. THE TENCTON PLANET (Germany): Wiessengrund 5, 48336, Laer, Germany.

There are, at present, the following Web sites devoted to different aspects of *Alien Nation* (please note that Internet Web sites frequently change their URLs):

Alien Nation Appreciation Society:
http://www.timg.demon.co.uk/anas.htm

Alien Nation Frequently Asked Questions:
http://home.interpath.net/pat/an/faq.html

Alien Nation FTP Site:
ftp://ftp.doc.ic.ac.uk/pub/media/tv/collections/tardis/us/sci-fi/AlienNation/

Alien Nation Links: http://www.visi.com/~wildfoto/a_nation.html

Dennis' Home Page:
http://www-public.tu-bs.de:8080/~y0003231/index.html

Gates of Bravo: http://bravo.flextech.co.uk/

German *Alien Nation* Page:
http://alf.zfn.uni-bremen.de/~taechl/falienati.htm

Jeff Lee's Home Page: http://www.gate.net/~shipbrk/tencton/

Little Tencton: http://www.ucinet.com/~snyder/index.html

Official Eric Pierpoint Web Page: http://www.scifinetwork.com/alien

Sci-Fi Channel: *Alien Nation*: http://www.scifi.com/aliennation/

Tim Gathercole's Home Page: http://www.timg.demon.co.uk/

For information about, and/or to join Internet e-mail listings devoted to *Alien Nation*, contact the following:

Click & Hum: debbien@netspace.net.au

Tencton-L: majordomo@mlists.com
[send with the message <subscribe Tencton-L>]

Tim Gathercole at tim@timg.demon.co.uk

Web Contact: wildfoto@visi.com

INDEX

ABOUT THE AUTHOR

Edward Gross has covered the film and television mediums for a wide variety of magazines, including *New York Nightlife*, *Comics Scene*, *Fangoria*, *SFX*, *The Island Ear*, *Starburst*, *Zap!*, *Premiere*, *Sci-Fi Universe*, *Dreamwatch*, and *Cinefantastique*. He was New York correspondent for *Starlog* and is currently senior editor at *Cinescape*.

He has also written a number of non-fiction books, among them *Secret File: The Making of Wiseguy*, *The 25th Anniversary Odd Couple Companion*, *The Dark Shadows Tribute Book*, *Growing Up in the Sixties: The Wonder Years*, *Rocky and the Films of Sylvester Stallone*, *Fab Films of the Beatles*, and, with Mark A. Altman, *Captains' Logs: The Complete Trek Voyages*, *Captains' Logs: Supplemental*, and *Trek Navigator*.

He lives on Long Island, New York, with his wife, Eileen, their sons Teddy, Dennis, and Kevin, a mutt named Clifford, and a really cool big-screen TV.